Schuylkill

Valley

Journal

Volume 45

Fall 2017

The *Schuylkill Valley Journal* is published twice a year

Patrons of the Schuylkill Valley Journal

(contributions of $50 or more)

Bill Ehrhart	Eric Greinke
Peter Krok	Zakiyah Kadry, MD
Claire Magee	Richard Krok
Bernadette McBride	Suzanne Marinell
Fran Metzman	Christine McKee
Robert Spreter	Richard Moyer
Bill Wunder	Shirley Wood

Subscriptions: Single Issue: 10 and $13 (if mailing is included)
1 year: $23 (includes mailing)
2 years: $45 (includes mailing)

Submissions: See page 200 for a complete list of guidelines.

Cover photo: Octavius Valentine Catto
Sculptor: Branly Cadet
Photographer: Ron Howard

Founding Editor	Jim Marinell
Publisher and Editor-in-Chief	Peter Krok
Managing Editor	Mark Danowsky
Co-Poetry Editor	Bill Wunder
Co-Poetry Editor	Bernadette McBride
Fiction Editor	Fran Metzman
Flash Fiction Editor	M.J. Iuppa
Arts Editor	David P. Kozinski
Staff Photographer	Ron Howard
Contributing Writer	Mike Cohen
Contributing Writer	Ray Greenblatt
Contributing Writer	Eric Greinke
Reader	Carolynn Kingyens
Production Editor/Layout Design	Ed Hart
Online Architect/Producer	Jordan Heil

The *Schuylkill Valley Journal* is available online at
www.svjlit.com

Contents
Volume 45, Fall 2017

Contents continued
Volume 45, Fall 2017

REMEMBERING A NEARLY FORGOTTEN HERO

by Mike Cohen

While sculptures all over our country are being moved, removed and, in some cases, abused, people in the City of Brotherly Love have come together to install a new statue. A recent addition to the bronze population of Philadelphia is a monument in the likeness of Octavius Catto. Of all the statues in the city, this (at long last) is the first to represent a specific named person of color. The dedication of a memorial to this man is not simply a case of affirmative action in public art. Catto, who lived from 1839 to 1871, was a teacher, orator, civil rights activist, community leader, and even a star baseball player. Octavius Catto accomplished all this in the short lifetime allotted him before he was killed by an assassin's bullet at the age of 32. The recognition is well-deserved and long overdue.

At age 15, Catto was a student at the Institute for Colored Youth, a school on Lombard Street in Philadelphia. Five years later, he was teaching math and English at that school. In 1861, Catto became the alumni association's first president. His leadership extended to the local branch of the Equal Rights League, the first national organization established (in 1864) for the promotion of human rights, especially the right to vote which was denied people of color.

The quest for civil rights began long before the Civil Rights Movement of the 1950's. In 1955, Rosa Parks famously refused to cede her seat on a bus to a white rider in Alabama where blacks were expected to move to the back of a bus in deference to white riders who would sit toward the front. Nearly a century earlier, Octavius Catto helped write the bill of legislation to provide people of color access to Philadelphia street cars, a law that was passed in 1867. At that time, Philadelphia public mass transit consisted of privately owned horse-drawn streetcars. Many of the owners did not allow people of color on the streetcars at all. Some would occasionally condescend to permit a black person to pay to board. That person would be relegated not to the back of the car, but to the front platform, an exposed position on the car subject to spattering by dirt from the street as well as dirt from the horse.

Access to public transportation was necessary to give people an opportunity for jobs that required travel to a work site, a right basic to daily life and to earning a living in the city. In March of 1867, after many unsuccessful attempts, the bill Octavius Catto helped to write was passed to make it illegal to deny streetcar access to black passengers in Pennsylvania.

There were restrictions to overcome in terms of recreation as well. Catto led the struggle to have the baseball team he founded, the Pythians, compete against white ball clubs. The appeal to have the Pythians admitted to the National Association of Amateur Base Ball Players was known to the delegates as "Catto's proposal." Unfortunately, the association refused.

On the other hand, the efforts of the Equal Rights League finally met with success in 1870 when Congress passed the fifteenth amendment to allow black men to vote. But legislation is only a step toward effecting social change. The 1871 mayoral election in Philadelphia pointed up the disparity between legislation and reality. There was major strife in our fair city at the time of the 1871 election. Local Democrats were resentful

^ Bas relief scenes from Catto's life;
< the 15th Amendment to the
U.S. Constitution

that their hold on the city might be broken by black voters who were likely to cast their ballots for the party of Abraham Lincoln—Republican. Rioting and violence erupted to discourage black voters from exercising their new right. National Guard troops were called upon to uphold the law. The Fifth Brigade, a black division of which Catto was a major, was among those called to duty. On his way to brigade headquarters, Octavius Catto was shot and killed for the cause he had fostered—martyred to that cause after its apparent success.

The idea for this memorial began more than a decade before the current controversy over statuary in the United States. This project was twelve years in the works. With the support of former Mayors John Street and Michael Nutter along with current Mayor Jim Kenney, the Catto statue has finally taken its place. The memorial was dedicated in a ceremony at Philadelphia's City Hall on September 26, 2017 before a large, enthusiastic crowd of citizens, including several of Catto's descendants.

Elements of "A Quest for Parity" by Branly Cadet— the installation at Philadelphia's City Hall honoring Octavius V. Catto

"There must come a change which shall force upon this nation that course which providence seems wisely to be directing for the mutual benefit of all peoples."

Sculptor Branly Cadet was chosen by a committee of artists to design and fashion the memorial to Octavius Catto. Earlier, Cadet had sculpted the twenty-one foot statue of Adam Clayton Powell, Jr., the first of New York's African American congressmen, that stands in front of the New York State Office Building. Another of Branly Cadet's works is the Jackie Robinson statue at Dodger Stadium in Los Angeles.

The Octavius Catto sculpture is at once grand and finely nuanced. The face of the statue shows both determination and dignity. The sculptural gesture is a total-body gesture, ambiguous with a dash of desperation, a smidgeon of supplication, a pinch of impatience, a flicker of frustration, and an ample amount of appeal to the humanity of humanity. You can almost hear Catto saying, "Why not simply respect one another? Is that really so difficult?"

References

https://whyy.org/episodes/monuments-in-philadelphia/ — Marty Moss-Coane interview with DAN BIDDLE and MURRAY DUBIN, authors of *Tasting Freedom: Octavius Catto and the Battle for Equality in Civil War America*, and PAUL FARBER, artistic director of Monument Lab and Managing Director of the Penn Program in the Environmental Humanities.

http://www.phillytrib.com/news/sculptor-reflects-on-octavius-v-catto-statue/article_74327f2a-4034-5b72-b590-befe2a3e2ccb.html

http://www.phillytrib.com/news/city-unveils-design-for-octavius-catto-memorial-statue/article_d86a293c-8e0a-5e78-b2a0-0bef5d959888.html

http://www.history.com/topics/black-history/civil-rights-movement

http://www.ushistory.org/catto/chap8-analyze.html

http://www.sfchronicle.com/giants/shea/article/Oakland-sculptor-s-statue-captures-Jackie-11110655.php

https://en.wikipedia.org/wiki/National_Equal_Rights_League

PENTTBOM

by Joseph Rathgeber

I rent Hani Hanjour's Paterson apartment. I don't mean to say he's the landlord; he's a prior tenant. You know him even if you don't think you do. Might as well say it plain. He was the hijacker of Flight 77. He piloted the Pentagon plane. He didn't live here long—five months, they estimate. It was only a weigh station, a home base. Not quite a headquarters. It was a pit stop—okay, the *last* stop—before the attacks. I guess he dressed and applied aftershave here before going to the airport. Showered, put on deodorant, combed his hair—that sort of thing. I wonder whether he used the same ice cube tray that's in the freezer, the one that was here when I moved in.

*

The rent's reasonable: $650 for a one-bedroom with an eat-in kitchen. You won't do much better in this area. It's on the top-floor of a three-story brick building, so I hover above the fray, view the sneakers tangled on telephone wires up-close, and only faintly hear the reggaeton rattling from the tricked-out Honda Civic parked on the street below. It hits me like a lullaby. Only the modified exhaust, like a deviated septum snore, awakens me as it finally pulls away in the wee hours.

*

I've got a minimum number of family members, even fewer friends, and none of them are conveniently located. I don't get many phone calls. This man is an island. I prefer it that way. I spend a lot of time alone, always have. My father once told me *People watch out for loners,* and, to be honest, the thought of being watched out for excites me. My landlord's not the type to run a background check, but if he were, my record would come up clean.

*

Rosa, my Puerto Rican neighbor, lives on the first floor. I know she's Puerto Rican because there's a flag hanging from her mailbox (which is really all of our mailboxes—one of those cluster jobs). It's a modest flag, parade spectator size. It's not obnoxious enough to complain about. She's also got a bumper sticker on her Buick that says *Boricua!*, but that's her business more than mine. I watch her Dominican ex-husband do his best

Stella shout every Saturday night. He pitches Johnnie Walker airport bottles sidearm into the sewer grate.

Rosa's who told me about Hani. The landlord never mentioned it, though you figure he'd be lawfully obligated to disclose information like that, like with a fire or a homicide. I was hauling groceries up the stairs, stocking my cabinets for the first time, when she grabbed my arm: "Terrorists lived in your apartment, y'know."

*

I decided to do my own research. I was nodding off while watching a classic rap video countdown on BET. Biggie's "Juicy" came in at number two. I never know if the ranking on these countdowns refers to the quality of the song or the quality of the video. The network censored the line *blow up like the World Trade*. This, I'm guessing, because they don't want to receive complaint letters, insensitivity to the victims and whatnot. Still, Biggie was talking about the 1993 truck bombing. It's not a reference to the big show of 2001.

They didn't censor the line with a bleep. They reversed it. It ended up sounding like a recording of paranormal activity in a haunted mental institution. I thought it was funny how BET felt obligated to retroactively label the lyric inappropriate. I took it all as a sign: the countdown, the video, the song, the lyric. I was sitting at my computer a few minutes later.

*

Rosa was always mentioning his name to me: Hani Hanjour. I put Hani's name in the search bar. Spelt it wrong, but the internet corrected it for me. I found biographical details collected by federal commissions and independent investigators. Here's what I gleaned.

Hani's life was full of false starts and setbacks. When he was a little boy he had dreams of becoming a flight attendant. He was aiming low, I guess. The flight attendant gig never panned out. His brother made fun of him, called him a *manyak*. The Arabic-English online translator tells me *manyak* means faggot in Arabic.

He set his sights on becoming a pilot instead—a more manly, and therefore acceptable, profession. He applied for a job with Saudi Arabian Airlines, but his grades weren't up to snuff. He knew if he could obtain a commercial pilot's license in the States he'd be golden. That was his next move.

Determined, Hani got accepted to the Sierra Academy of Aeronautics in California. He was lucky enough to stay with a host family in Oakland. This was in May 1996. He struggled through an ESL class but had to withdraw from the academy before receiving any pilot training. He couldn't afford the tuition.

Hani moved to Phoenix, enrolled in a much cheaper flight school based out of Scottsdale, but flunked out. He was on a flight back to Saudi Arabia by November. No pilot's license to speak of.

Fast forward three years. Hani returns to the States—his English stronger and his focus keener, and he earns the coveted FAA commercial pilot's license. He gets a "satisfactory" rating, which isn't an A+, more like a B. Hani hightails it back to Saudi Arabia, applies to Saudi Arabian Airlines for the second time—the clincher, he believes—only to be rejected again. Crushed, Hani becomes withdrawn, takes on other interests, and leaves his family without warning. Here, the timeline gets sketchy. But he eventually ends up high-stepping through tires and hanging from monkey bars at a training camp in Afghanistan.

*

He died at twenty-nine. I learned that, too. That's the age I was when I learned it. It spooked me. It spooked me like seeing ectoplasm in an old family portrait. I felt like I was being haunted.

I thought of my twenty-nine-year-old face and wanted to see his. I did a Google image search and came up with a few. First one I found was a headshot. He had facial hair not unlike mine: shaped-up tight on the chin and around the mouth, the look of an R&B singer. He looked handsome.

The next image was a surveillance camera still from an ATM machine. There's a timestamp in the top left corner, too blurry to make out. This image was collected by the authorities after the attacks. It's Hani and another guy. They look cool and collected, both wearing collared button-downs. The image is reminiscent of how rappers—especially duos—would pose, tilting their heads forward a bit, eyes looking up, and with a fisheye lens effect. It reminded me of a full-page ad in *The Source*.

Next I found an image of the apartment Hani stayed in, which is to say, an image of my apartment. It was a street-level view of the place, taken on a sunny day, probably late August or early September. It had the oversaturated look of an Indian summer. Staring at the image of our apartment gave me the willies.

There I was in front of my computer, staring at an image of the building I'm sitting in—yep, right through that third-story window. It's like that hand drawing a hand drawing a hand drawing. Like a mirror held up to a mirror. It was that foundationless deal where there's no bottom. Kind of like the chicken and egg dilemma. The image had me questioning causality. But I stopped the line of causality when it came down to questioning whether the Wright Brothers were to blame for Hani's attack.

I ended up staring at a satellite image of the United States at night. The image showed the density of ground lights. North Jersey was a blanket white splotch, alit with human activity.

*

The following morning I woke up annoyed. I was bothered by the frequent two *t* misspelling of Paterson on message boards and user forums—all these opinions about Hani, about my adopted city, about our apartment. "One *t* in Paterson," I kept muttering as I brushed my teeth, as I showered. I muttered as if giving voice to the error would correct it.

*

I felt hung over from my research. I needed a meal. I also needed to be around people, for once. I needed to ask what they knew about Hani.

I footed it down to the Egg Platter for breakfast. It's a rundown trailer, all chrome and peeling wallpaper, that boasts twenty-one varieties of eggs. I ordered a western omelet and got comfy on a stool, comfy as a stool gets. Feeling like an investigative journalist, I asked the old man sitting two stools down—one of Paterson's residual Italians—if he knew anything about Hani. "One of the terrorists," I had to clarify. "…that lived here for awhile."

The geezer mumbled something about "dune coons" and got real fidgety on his stool. He paid his bill and hurried out. There were still hash browns on his plate. I felt guilty that my question made him exit so abruptly. I felt bad about the uneaten hash browns on his plate.

*

My research went on for consecutive nights. I read long reports. I wanted to know more than the cliffnotes version of Hani's life. I wanted to know more about the time he spent in the apartment.

One of Hani's neighbors was interviewed by the *Star-Ledger* and claimed Hani knocked on his door one evening asking how to screw in a light bulb. "He seemed clueless," the neighbor said.

This anecdote didn't strike me as trustworthy. The incident didn't seem likely, didn't seem real. It seemed too tailor-made for internet jokes.

How many terrorists does it take to screw in a light bulb? It seems designed to belittle.

*

The Egg Platter keeps wacky hours. It's open from 10PM to 3PM. They cater to the trucker crowd, the teenage drunks, the nighthawks. I went in at 4AM, unable to sleep. I couldn't keep Hani out of my head.

I ordered scrambled eggs and started a conversation with the guy next to me. This interviewee was friendlier, with more to say. He was also an Arab—Palestinian, he said. He didn't recognize Hani by name, but when I said the word terrorist he went off.

"This is where they claimed we celebrated," he said, referring to Paterson (one *t*). "Between Main and Getty. In and around the Triangle park off Eagle. South Paterson. I say *claimed* because it was all bullshit, man. Eyewitness accounts completely unsubstantiated. *Unsubstantiated* is too weak a word. They were falsehoods, media-generated rumors. I can speak on it because I was there. No one was stomping on American flags. Nobody was chanting DEATH TO AMERICA! Nobody was ululating— nobody. No hooting, no hollering.

"I tell you what though…" He searched for my name, but I hadn't given it to him. "The Palestinians of South Paterson were very much *unlike* the Hasidim who danced around the grave of their 'martyr' Baruch Goldstein, if you ask me. What it boils down to is this: the media wanted a domestic version of what they captured and broadcast over and over again, on a loop: a handful of yokels in East Jerusalem—mostly kids— bribed to dance for the camera. Arafat put the kibosh on that. He shut that down quick. That doesn't reflect the majority opinion of Palestin- ians," he said.

"Now you say you live in a terrorist apartment. So what? Do you think it's a curse? A bogeyman? Don't you know most the apartments in North Jersey have been rented by killers? Mafioso boss-man Sam the Plumber sold pipes and fittings out of a store in Kenilworth. Centu- ries ago the Lenni Lenape were slaughtered by the white man on these grounds. Terrible shit happens everywhere is my point. It doesn't mean my sister should be subjected to taunts of *jihad jihad* and *Allahu Akbar* when she walks into a bank wearing a hijab."

He was riled up. I thanked him for his time. I left my scrambled eggs cold and unfinished on my plate.

*

Feeling as though my interviews were going nowhere, I broke night doing research on the internet again. I found out that many—if not most—of the terrorists frequented my apartment. At the very least they paid it a courtesy visit. There were brothers Nawaf and Salem. There was Majed, Ahmed, and Abdulaziz. Khalid stopped over once, escorted by Mohamed. This is how I came to know them, on a first-name basis.

The article that outlined the list of guests—Hani's visitors—was penned by a neocon, a conspiracy theorist, a sixteen-year-old boy, or some combination thereof. The author of the article referred to this group of terrorists as the Arab Rat Pack.

I sat at my computer fantasizing about them. I saw them huddled around a table, playing cards. I saw them holding hands during a séance, candles and incense burning on a lazy susan. I saw them with maps, airline tickets, business cards, and minute-by-minute agendas, plotting the attacks, the apartment full of cigarette smoke. I saw slumber bags on the floor. One of them was sprawled on the couch. It was almost like a slacker apartment, or a frat house. There was laundry strewn everywhere. There was a tall bottle of Vaseline Intensive Care lotion on the tank of the toilet bowl. There they were. In the flesh. There they were in my living room: a cadre. There they were: a cell.

*

I was on my way to the Egg Platter, thinking about the menu, thinking eggs benedict. I detoured and came to the Straight & Narrow building on the corner of Straight and Narrow. An addict, or a recovering addict, or a bum, was sitting on a stack of cinderblocks outside. He called me over.

"Look at this shit, brother. Look at it. You think that's coincidence?"

He held a sullied and folded twenty dollar bill in front of my face. The folds were folded in such a way that I was staring at the Towers engulfed in two puffs of smoke.

"Yeah, probably," I answered.

"Ahh, you're a blind man," he said. "You're blind." He waved me off and approached the next man.

I pulled a dollar bill from my wallet. I squinted to find the owl in the upper right corner and then folded the bill to transform George Washington's hair into the face of a monkey. I unfolded the bill and winked at the all-seeing eye atop the pyramid. That bum had a twenty, I thought as I walked off. I did the math. He could afford ten meals at the Egg Platter with that.

*

A couple nights later, I fell asleep on my couch and had my most vivid dream of Hani yet.

I'm on my couch watching television. It's Christmas Eve. I'm watching what I figure is a John Lennon music video, even though I'm pretty sure John Lennon never made a music video. John is playing "Imagine" on a white piano in a white room. The set designer must've been trying to create the heaven of the lyrics, even though the lyric goes *Imagine there's no heaven.* Never mind the *no*, right?

Yoko appears. She's pulling back white curtains that reveal a view of a white patio and a white garden. All the plants and flowers are albino. The view is momentary. White light floods the white room, and I see Hani in ectoplasm form appear above Yoko's head.

I've got my hand in a bag of burnt microwave popcorn, listening to John sing about peace, and a brick comes crashing through my window. It lands on the floor equidistant between me and the TV. It has a note rubberbanded around it. Hani appears on my couch. He bounces closer and throws his arm around me. He's going on about how us Americans were right, the 72 virgins racket was a bust. He's begging me to take him to the strip club for some poon-tang (his term, not mine). I guess I can drop you off at the Hitching Post, I say. *Drop me off? You're coming with,* Hani says. *Let's get fucking wasted!*

I point to the brick on the floor in front of us. We've got to take care of that first, I say. I pick up the brick and unwrap the note from it. The note's laminated. I unfold it but can't read it. It's written in Arabic. I ask Hani to read it. *I can't read that shit,* he says. *C'mon, let's get some pussy!*

My patience with Hani is dwindling. He's so immature. You don't come across like this in the reports, I tell him. He's ignoring me. He's at the mirror tucking in his collared button-down. I tell him, We've got to handle this brick note before we do anything or go anywhere. He huffs like he's about to throw a tantrum. Then he says: *Well try to see who threw it, dummy.*

We stand side-by-side with our heads out the broken apartment window. To the neighborhood, we look like two babushkas. It's like we're sharing the same set of eyes. We see the tricked-out Honda Civic and Rosa's Buick with the *Boricua!* bumper sticker. We see a young, black kid running in slow-motion around the corner. All we can make out are his legs kicking up behind him. His sneakers are the same sneakers that hang on the telephone wires outside our window. The legs and the sneakers freeze. It's as though somebody hit pause on the VCR. Hani and I turn to each other. He gazes into my eyes like he wants to kiss me. We turn our attention back out the window and suddenly we're 90-some-odd stories up. The legs of our suspect are ant-size. His sneakers, ant antennae. The skyscraper heights make me dizzy. I collapse on the couch, hit with a touch of vertigo. Hani holds a cold compress to my forehead.

*

My analysis of the dream? I'm not much for dream interpretations. Having a book of dream meanings in my nightstand seems worthless. Dream of spiders and there's manipulation happening in your life. What's to be gained from that? I might as well read my horoscope.

I do acknowledge that dreams include recollections from your waking hours, though. And I can explain away John Lennon. In my research, I read that a ban list went into effect for all radio stations after the attacks—a list of songs that could not, under any circumstances, be played. The FCC distributed the memo.

Topping the list? John's "Imagine." Why? The FCC didn't include explanations. But the next link I clicked brought me to a quote from John, circa sometime around the release of the single. He said the song was "an anti-religious, anti-nationalistic, anti-conventional, anti-capitalistic tune." There's a pause—represented in print with an ellipsis—then an afterthought. "Because it's sugarcoated, it's accepted."

*

I was all egged out. I shoveled some waffles in the toaster oven instead. At some point in my investigation sleep became secondary, an afterthought. My research was dominating my nights and now my days, too. I blew off a job fair and missed a dental appointment. They billed me a cancellation fee. Did I mention I started to relish the thought of receiving an overdue bill, or a Macy's catalog, or a free nickel from the Leukemia & Lymphoma Society with Hani's name printed on the envelope? I wanted to forward his mail to him. Like I wanted to believe he filled the same ice cube tray as me, held it under the same tap, plopped the same hard water cubes into a glass.

I was reading over Hani's Wikipedia page again. I scrolled past his photo ID-cum-mug shot, past his role in the attacks, and re-read his biography. His false starts. His setbacks. His failures. I was reading about his straight F report card from the flight school in Scottsdale again when I said *enough!* and decided to alter the entry.

*

Mr. Hanjour excelled in his flight school classes while in Arizona, I typed. *Mr. Hanjour wowed his instructors and immediately received a job offer from Continental Airlines*. I typed *Mr. Hanjour passed all his assessments with flying colors.*

The entry was cold and dispassionate, so I created a Personal Life section, too. *Mr. Hanjour was devoted to his family*, I typed. *He enjoyed American cuisine like southwestern spicy buffalo wings. His favorite film was* Airplane!

I saved my edits, closed the browser window, opened it again, and returned to the page. My edits were there. I refreshed the page. Like doing a double-take, I needed to be sure my changes remained. They did. Satisfied, I took a well-earned nap.

When I woke up, I booted up the computer and returned to the page. Some anonymous user had fucked with my changes. He questioned the validity of my contribution. In brackets and superscript at the end of my flight school sentence was added *citation needed*. There was an insulting *source?* after every detail in my Personal Life section. The italics gave me the impression this anonymous editor was a real know-it-all. I slammed my mouse.

Okay, I thought—I probably shouldn't have used "wowed" or "with flying colors." The writing wasn't polished enough. I told myself to wait a couple weeks and then revise my contributions. These future plans didn't calm me, though. I was pissed.

I scrolled to the section of the page that lists the timeline of events leading up to the attacks. I located the part that mentions the Paterson apartment. I changed *Patterson* to *Paterson*. I placed my cursor at the end of the apartment address: 486 Union Avenue.

I held down the backspace key.

486 Union…

486…

48…

4….

.

I deleted Hani's address—deleted *my* address, *our* address—from the page. I clicked save. I made it like the apartment didn't exist. The apartment didn't exist.

*

Hani appeared in my dreams consecutive nights. My sleep schedule was so irregular that I couldn't distinguish between waking dreams, or visions, or hallucinations. I wasn't lucid. I couldn't distinguish between day and night. I got in the habit of keeping the curtains drawn.

In most of the dreams Hani is ectoplasm, a straight-up ghost, his body diaphanous in the light of the computer monitor. Lately he's a different Hani than the Hani from the John Lennon dream. Now he's always a stoical Hani. Contrary to the official reports that mock Hani's grasp of the English language, ghost Hani speaks perfectly—enunciates every word. He's a regular linguist. But he speaks inches from my face, too close. I feel his breath like a warm draft. No regard for personal space. He struggles with slang. For example, he didn't understand how *fly* could mean to move through the air and also to be dressed in a cool way. It was on me to explain the slang to him.

*

TV puts me to sleep. It's the only thing that seems to work. My waking hours, my alert hours, are time spent away from Hani. I don't so much "watch" TV as sit in front of the set allowing the screen's glow to illuminate my face in the pitch black apartment. I watch on mute. I channel surf until I find something that interests me, which is usually nothing.

BET is replaying the classic rap video countdown. What else is there to broadcast at the ungodly hour of 4AM? The countdown is at number four (Dre and Snoop's "Nuthin' but a 'G' Thang") when I turn it on. The host throws to commercial after every video. Dre is followed by one of those *the few, the proud, the Marines* commercials. There's footage of helicopters, parachutes, and mud-caked faces grimacing through the boot camp rope climb. The subtitles include the phrase *patriotic music playing* squeezed between two music notes.

Number three is Ice Cube's "It Was a Good Day." *Today I didn't even have to use my AK*, I rap as they cut to another commercial break. I slouch to the kitchen and grab a bottle of NyQuil from the cabinet above the sink. I slump onto the couch, break the children's seal on the bottle, and take several swigs.

Biggie's "Juicy" is up next, as expected. I read the subtitles at the bottom of the screen. I await the controversial World Trade line, curious if it will be censored in subtitles just as it was in audio. The subtitles appear and vanish at a rapid pace, playing catch-up. I imagine a stenographer crouched inside my TV trying to keep up with Biggie's lyrics.

When the line arrives, I'm watching Biggie's mouth—reading his lips—at the same time I'm reading the subtitles. They censor it. They put an ellipsis in its place. I expected it to be censored, but I expected a row of asterisks, not a humdrum row of periods. I shut off the TV.

I climb into bed disappointed and, admittedly, a little lonesome. My investigation has reached a dead-end. There's nobody left to interview. My internet research is going nowhere: all links clicked, all reports read. There's nothing redeemable about life lately, I think. Only Hani. Hani's all I've got. I promise never to leave this apartment, our apartment. I will always pay the rent on time. No eviction notice will ever be glued to the door. Instead of saying a bedtime prayer, I make a wish: that Hani will appear tonight. I need him more than ever.

*

Hani snuggles up next to me. We spoon. Hani whispers sweet nothings in my ear and puts his hand down the front of my flannel pants. Sade's "Smooth Operator" starts playing on the stereo. Hani tells me his success story from start to finish, his voice soft and breathy. He tells me how he learned English with flashcards, how he aced all his tests in flight school. He tells me how he used to be a wing walker on a biplane in Texas and how he made ends meet as a barnstormer. He explains how he wasn't part of a terrorist cell but of a flying circus. He made my inner ear moist with his résumé and his accolades. He says he was star of the airshow, his stunts renowned from coast to coast. He did loop-the-loops and barrel rolls and dives. He even flew an F-18 fighter jet over the Super Bowl. All this, he says, and all anyone ever talks about is the Pentagon.

Author's Note

"PENTTBOM" is the codename for the FBI's investigation into the September 11 attacks of 2001. I became somewhat obsessed with the investigation when I discovered several of the hijackers had rented an apartment not far from my house. That proximity made me want to discover the human side of one of these terrorists—not rely simply on the caricatured, reductive portrayal as related to a heinous act. So, like the FBI, I investigated Hani Hanjour's life, albeit fictively.

ROADSIDE ARREST

by Peter Kuklinski

The beginning of my story is a silly re-run looping inside my psyche—one of those extraneous but hardwired memories that withstands time. Perhaps a testament to childhood impressions overtaking new memories as time slides forward? You cannot easily see the *Dennis the Menace* series nowadays without digging for it, but little help this does me.

I watched an episode in 1972 when I was ten in which Dennis captures a gopher from the other side of town and releases it next door in "good old" Mr. Wilson's garden. Mr. Wilson, that uptight, fussy, consummate gardener, is enraged with the appearance of a gopher burrowing among his prized beds—a varmint that had not been seen on his side of town in more than twenty years.

Mr. Wilson reacts with zany measures to rid his yard of the pest and true to form, he becomes more and more frustrated as he fails.

From that point onward I adopted Mr. Wilson's opinion that gophers, or groundhogs as they are also commonly called, are strictly pests and varmints. Only an unusual intersection of events changed this perspective for me, forever. So it's not surprising then that I am outraged with the sighting of one such rodent in my own backyard.

I tear out the backdoor to rescue my yelping and beloved Shih Tzu-Bichon pooch, Coco, from tangling with the invader about her size, but way more wildlife savvy-superior. Upon my rush, the gopher plunges into a hole under my shed which looks way small for it to make it through, but it does so with grace. It then peeps out at me through a trellis that covers the space between the ground and the shed's floor, like it's mocking me. It just stands there as I peer into its dark eyes. I fear for Coco that I will not be on hand during the next encounter. I yell and kick at the trellis until the gopher finally retreats, albeit unhurriedly, which pisses me off.

Now I become like an enraged farmer with a tilted tractor in his field as I survey the numerous holes throughout my yard. I fill them with gravel and into several places along the back fence I shove bricks and even cinder block chunks in two of the largest entry points burrowing below the fence. New holes appear a few days later, so I call an exterminator, who informs me of their ten-day backlog due to a stink bug wave. An estimate of three hundred dollars for the pending service is quoted. The damage to my yard, the threat to Coco, and the impact on my wallet.... fuels a fire in my heart to rid myself of this nuisance.

This is when I decide to do the job myself. I own an air rifle from my adolescent years and believe that I am still a good shot. My pump action single load pellet rifle is standing in the back of a closet, even though I haven't fired it for years. It's stationed perpetually on hand for the day when I might need it which turns out to be today.

I'm upstairs when I spot the invader waddling in my yard over pieces of acorn shells. I retrieve my rifle. Its smooth walnut stock feels cool and strong. I live in a more urbanized suburban community where air rifles are against the law to use. I counter this opposing tenet with two more pressing facts. One, I'm not a reckless, adolescent plinker; and two, a controlled shot is clearly my best solution. The local authorities even employ controlled shooting techniques to battle an over population of deer within a nearby city park. This justification is enough for me to pump six strokes and create a ready force equating approximately 715 feet per second for the 5 mm pellet—a wallop that will end my problem.

As I aim at its small head from about 30 feet away, I hear my wife coming toward me. She is a law abiding animal lover, so killing vermin in our yard and disposing of it under her witness is a messy affair best avoided. For one, she never hunted small game in isolated woods like the Jeremiah Johnson wannabe I was in junior high school, and two, I am not up to explaining it all to her. Nine years of marriage taught me that much. I hold off until it is clear and I return to my post only to find that the rascal had absconded.

I keep my rifle hidden but easily accessible, and loaded with the safety activated as I patrol the yard from the upstairs windows whenever I can. Becoming a sentry feels natural for I am protecting my family and property and am well within my rights to exercise earnest dissent from societal norms. It feels very American, even patriotic.

Tomorrow comes. It's early Sunday morning and my wife is away at the gym. Bingo! I spot the chubby invader across the road. A perfect situation because it will appear as if it was clipped by a passing car, of which there are often many zipping by. I ready myself to take a clear shot, glancing up and down the street twice from my upstairs perch to make sure there are no cars. It's quieter on Sunday mornings and I am confident of imminent success. I aim but the bugger moves so I pause and readjust my aim twice before a clear shot is at hand. The moment I finally squeeze the trigger, a flash heading straight into my line of fire enters my peripheral vision. It turns out to be a bicyclist at high speed zipping down the long hill parallel to my house. I didn't hear anything. My squeeze, by the time of this profound revelation, is un-retractable. The splat from the shot melts in the tsunami of dread overwhelming me as I watch the bicyclist crash about ten yards past the gopher. I lose sight of the gopher as the bicyclist's brightly colored form tumbles onto the middle of the street. A speeding trucker not far behind her screeches the brakes and I involuntarily squeeze my eyes shut under fast mangling and thumping sounds. It is like an unbalanced and overloaded washer on a spin cycle bouncing in a march of thumps. I heave and hold onto to the door jamb not to fall down. By the time I make it outside, two cars are stopped and frantic mobile phone conversations are taking place. It feels like a tragic movie and I'm the leading man. The biker is twisted, bloody… motionless. She…it's even a she. She is not wearing a helmet and her ashen blonde hair is fanned on the asphalt. I am so scared that I retreat and watch from afar. Cops and ambulances fill the street. Within two hours, they are gone. I remain alone in the garage…petrified. What remains is a dark pool spot from her blood that is smeared along its edges.

The television news reports that Rose Haldeman lost control of her bicycle and crashed causing an unavoidable impact from a young driver of a trailing truck cruising well above the speed limit. The bicyclist is killed instantly by not wearing a helmet. I read a similar report in the next morning's newspaper. A foundation to promote bicycle safety is invigorated with a new campaign in Rose Haldeman's honor. A phone number and web address for donations and membership are featured on television and in the newspaper. I am forever guilty without any chance for parole.

Rose Haldeman's friends and family erect a colorful memorial. Flowers and stuffed animals surround a cross with her name on it. The night they erect it, there are well over forty people holding candles. She must have been a good person. I am compelled to cross the street under the safety of a police officer guiding traffic, and join them in the rear of a tender vigil that makes me cry.

Often that weird thump of the truck hitting her plays in my head and it's impossible to put it out of my mind.

After several months, fewer people visit the memorial, then none. This is when I take over. The least I could do is maintain her memorial. I have to be careful crossing the street though, especially during rush hour. My wife wonders why I have taken such a keen interest in this memorial. I only say, "So she will not be forgotten."

One morning, I sight some litter within Rose's little alcove, so I hustle over to tidy up, like I always do. I clean up and soon begin to head back home, looking to and fro for oncoming traffic when a loud thrashing sound from a nearby bush startles me. I turn and gaze upon the largest gopher I have ever seen. It's standing upon its hind legs like a statue not more than a yard from me. I jump into the street and am instantly whacked with a huge impact. That loud familiar thump fills my ears and then the shrill screech of brakes and tires are the last things I recall as I fly into darkness toward the dense thicket bordering Rose's memorial. The other image flashing in my mind's eye is Mr. Wilson and the gopher in his yard.

Author's Note

In writing *Roadside Arrest*, I was struck by how an early impression can inform present circumstances, possibly leading to a bad decision and even dire consequences. Such an outcome is better avoided by sharing an emotional mindset reaction with another person who may offer a different and more successful path toward solving a problem.

THE GRAVITY OF FLOATING

by Marilyn L.T. Klimcho

The year I turned nine and my little sister turned seven Aunt Sally took us, two of her many nieces, to a pond a short trot from her house. Aunt Sally wanted to introduce us to a wonderful concept from her childhood: the swimming hole. This was the 1950s. I'm pretty sure it was before the invention of swimming pools, but just after the invention of elastic, bathing suits and modesty or I believe we would have encountered this pleasure either in our underwear or buck naked.

My sister and I donned matching polka dot suits and padded barefoot along the dirt path after Aunt Sally towards a muddy depression in the middle of a field of stubble.

Aunt Sally was a large woman who had given birth to five boys in an attempt to replicate the huge family that she had enjoyed growing up in as a child. At nine years of age I guessed that she was laboring under the delusion that having a girl would finally make parenthood worthwhile.

Not having any daughters yet, Aunt Sally had searched among the numerous children spawned by her nine brothers and sisters and settled upon the two of us to fulfill her needs. This must have been just before the invention of birth control.

Having huge families is not in vogue nowadays but in my grandmother's generation, having ten, fifteen or twenty kids was an economic necessity. That was the era of the family farm, and though my grandmother did not own a farm, she did have enough children to fully man eight farms.

Each of my grandmother's children grew up and married, thereby doubling the number of people jamming themselves into her tiny house during get-togethers. And those married couples reproduced a score or more of cousins, my playmates.

As a family we gathered often at my grandparents' house to gorge on potato salad, fried chicken, Swedish meatballs, deviled eggs, homemade breads, macaroni salad, Jell-o salad, apple, peach, cherry, blueberry and strawberry pies, cakes, brownies, potato chips, soda and iced tea. The events generated warmth in both the heart and the gut.

With that much closely related flesh packed into one house, there was jostling and teasing, joking and laughter. There was a cloud of cigar, cigarette and pipe smoke coming from the living room where my uncles cloistered with my grandfather. There were wonderful smells of rich foods and sounds of chatter coming from the kitchen where my aunts clustered around my grandmother.

I loved to install myself in the doorway between those two rooms and absorb the atmosphere of both.

Even at nine I grasped Aunt Sally's desire to recreate the camaraderie she found in her family of origin and I understood her plight when halfway through this monumental effort she had not produced a single daughter. I sympathized. She was overwhelmed by all of that testosterone. Something was going horribly wrong.

By the time the oldest boy had reached his teens Aunt Sally's kids were being approached by Planned Parenthood to pose as poster children with the caption, Don't Let THIS Happen to YOU. The boys ran about Aunt Sally's house yelling, jumping off of furniture, wrecking everything they touched, consuming huge amounts of junk food and reading large numbers of comic books.

They made so much commotion on any given day that Aunt Sally's standard parenting technique was to bellow, "Take it outside!" even if it was the dead of winter and the height of a blizzard.

To make her point stick with her rambunctious sons, Aunt Sally had an impressive set of lungs backed up by a massive, well-padded frame and a meaty right arm with the same grip King Kong used while he clung to the Empire State Building and fought off all of those fragile little planes.

Aunt Sally was a woman, with a capital W, a force of nature. I admired her. She had volunteered to tutor me and my dumb sister in the fine art of swimming. I couldn't wait. I'd never been swimming before and neither had my sister. We arrived at the pond. Her boys plunged in. It looked so easy! In minutes they were floating out in the center of the pond, diving, doing tricks and trying to submerge each other.

We were, in contrast to my rambunctious worldly cousins, being raised by shy retiring people who viewed physical activity of any kind and emotion of any depth with great alarm. In comparison with my Aunt Sally's house, mine could have been a nunnery. Hence, we were ninnies.

I was, however, an adventurous ninny, so when we reached the pond, I strode out across the mud until I stood chest deep in water, my feet precariously perched on the rocky bottom. With all my strength, I lifted my arms, flung myself forward and flailed.

My sister walked out ankle deep, slipped on some slimy rocks, put her head under the surface and began to drown by not trying to stand up.

What a ninny.

Aunt Sally, Colossus that she was, waded out and picked my sister up, whacked her on the back and plunked her on the shore to splutter and dry out.

That as a nine-year-old I even knew the word Colossus, the name of a huge ancient statue of a god towering over a harbor, was due to the World Book Encyclopedia. At home I would sit for hours and thumb the pages of that massive set of books, looking at prints of John the Baptist's head on a platter, the drawing of Joseph Haydn's wife cutting up his priceless musical scores for curling paper to do her hair and photos of the statue of Medusa with all of those snakes writhing upon her head.

I was quickly earning myself a classical education while my cousins in Aunt Sally's house were learning the fine arts of arson, breaking and entering and hot-wiring cars.

Despite her size and force of personality, my Aunt Sally and her husband could not control their five sons. Since he was away often, driving a truck, it fell upon Aunt Sally to manage on her own.

She expressed her frustration by the way she got red in the face and bellowed, but she was not embittered or resentful. Though Aunt Sally was not a particularly patient person, it was not because she expected her lot in life to improve. Indeed, except for wanting a daughter, she was content. Like a creature born and bred in a cage, she knew and accepted the boundaries of her life.

For example, as they grew older, it became a given that when they each reached their eighteenth birthday, the local police would park on Aunt Sally's street, waiting like fishermen on the first day of trout season for the moment when her sons were legal to catch and keep in jail. I'm happy to say that each one of them turned into a delightful criminal, complete with a rap sheet and prison tats. As a family we had both in-laws and real outlaws.

Another mother might have railed against fate, schemed against the system, fought with authorities or signed petitions. Aunt Sally sighed and said, "Well, then."

Lest you think my cousins were a total drain upon society with no redeeming value, I must point out that these boys endowed me and my sister with comic books. This was by way of a third party, my grandmother, who was the recipient of this treasure trove following Aunt Sally's periodic house purges.

Ensconced in my grandmother's rocking chair during our family's weekly visits, I could outgrow my regressive upbringing. I could become somebody.

The comics were a godsend. In school, I was dangerously close to becoming a teacher's pet and a pesky know-it-all. To counteract that, I kept putting out a lot of effort to be just like everyone else, to be normal, but every time I tried, I overshot the mark. What was I doing wrong? I would have become that most despised creature, a benighted nerd, but for my Aunt Sally, who left stacks of fresh comic books every time she visited her mother. Having been fed a steady diet of children's classics, I was starved for anything remotely popular.

Comic books were the next best thing to movies which I was too deeply embedded in the countryside to see very often. Superman took me on flights around the world. Batman led me down pitch dark alleys after criminals and taught me that only crazy people break the law. Aquaman took me swimming with whales and dolphins and let me visit submarines. The Green Arrow taught me archery, which I practiced diligently if ineffectually with notched sticks and cotton string. The Thing taught me the importance of being gentle.

I lived for Friday night visits to my grandmother's house and those stacks and stacks of comic books.

One Friday evening, a year after the near-drowning of my sister, I was reading about Batman's adventures at my grandmother's house when Aunt Sally lumbered into the living room. I was holed up in Grandmother's rocking chair, half way through a well-thumbed comic.

Aunt Sally was a good deal heavier than the last time I'd seen her. She was rounder around the middle. Our paths had crossed during the intervening time, but we'd not been alone together since the invitation to spend a weekend during which, despite my fondest wish and grandest efforts, I had not learned how to swim.

I looked up at Aunt Sally, but went back to Batman, turning pages rapidly. I was a pretty fast reader. The Joker had my hero cornered. I must have been totally engrossed, for I only gradually became aware that Aunt Sally had paused and was squinting at me. Was she unaware of my addiction to Superman, Green Arrow and The Thing?

I lowered the comic book.

Why was she giving me the hairy eyeball? It was true that studying in school was not among her family's cherished traditions, but surely reading comic books wasn't out of bounds. Her kids did it all of the time.

Aunt Sally said, "Do you always swim against the current?"

I found myself tongue tied. Aunt Sally was the one person I should be able to relax with. There was no pressure from her, no pretense, no need to meet high expectations. She never placed huge demands upon her children, yet at her utterance of these simple words and their implied criticism, I discovered that this woman, who embodied my vision of the ideal mother, did not trust me and I, like Adam and Eve, was about to repeat that greatest moment in all of human history: expulsion from the Garden of Eden.

Despite my extensive vocabulary, at ten, I did not have the sophistication necessary to express all of my complex feelings. You see, as a two-year-old, right after my wimpy sister was born, I deemed myself suddenly put out of a job. I was no longer the Chosen One, the undisputed center of my mother's universe.

I questioned both of my parents at length. Why had I been replaced in their affections? Had I cried excessively? Had I failed at thumb sucking? Had I bombed at cuteness? Were they unhappy with my work in general or was it something specific? I offered to do better. But it had all been to no avail. They would not return the baby to the hospital and I became a Big Sister.

Now here was Aunt Sally, a woman in search of a daughter. She had a vacant spot in her heart where I could snuggle. I could be the Shining One, the one Aunt Sally loved and petted.

Was I not the daughter she had longed for after all?

My heart sank. If I wasn't capable of filling this role, I wasn't capable of filling the role of favorite daughter in any family. Had I hatched from a cuckoo's egg? Had Aunt Sally recognized that I did not belong? Had I done something wrong? Was that why she looked like she didn't trust me?

I opened my mouth to voice a protest, but at that moment Grandmother called out from the kitchen, "Sally!" and Aunt Sally said, "Wh-a-t?"

in that sustained alto note of annoyance and bother at any interruption of her chosen course of action.

And so our moment passed and thus I, though I did not know it at the time, officially cast off the last line holding me back from entering the land of adulthood. I was forced to grow up. A few months later I heard that Aunt Sally gave birth to a baby girl.

Over the next twelve years I became familiar with fellow students exhibiting the same hesitant reaction to me that I'd discovered first in my mother and then in Aunt Sally. They'd see the effort I put into appearing normal and look at me as if I were the most clueless person they had ever met. Gradually they gave me a wider and wider berth.

From high school I fled to college, and when I finally returned home as an articulate young woman, my grandmother said in amazement that she'd never seen two people change as much as my sister and I did after we graduated from high school.

Jobs, marriage and children all fell in line. Even grandchildren eventually came along.

Then in my sixty-third year, the call went out and word spread. There would be a gathering of the clan. There would be a picnic. There had been many picnics over the years, and I had attended them all, but as my grandparents died off and then some of my aunts and uncles, the gatherings had become less frequent. Aunt Sally was organizing this year's event.

Aunt Sally had grown gray and grown lame. Her kids had settled down, left lives of crime to the ingenuity of younger folks and become parents themselves. Her eldest even went to the extra effort of having a huge family, nine in all, just to carry on the tradition of having big families. The rest of my cousins, me included, were noticeably reluctant to follow suit.

Orders went out regarding the picnic.

Bring a covered dish! Bring lawn chairs! Bring mosquito repellent! Bring your kids! Bring your grandkids! Bring a donation towards the pavilion rental! Aunt Ruth would go to the grounds ahead of time and set up tables and claim grills. Uncle Tom would start the charcoal fires going.

The day of the picnic dawned bright and sunny.

Cars with far-flung license plates streamed into the lot and people I hadn't seen in years sauntered over with dishes heaped with food until the park was a sea of cousins, aunts and uncles, with grandkids and great grandkids in tow, underfoot or in arms.

The picnic gathered steam.

There was chatter, laughter and teasing, all that catching up to do, a processional around the altar of food, then eating and a second processional around the dessert table.

Smiles of satisfaction grew on my cousins' faces; the joy of being immersed in a gathering of that many people, that much closely related flesh, all at the same location with that much food!

I was having a great time.

Things were winding down when Aunt Ruth cornered me and the two of us compared lives. She showed me pictures of her grandchildren and great-grandchildren. I showed her pictures of my first grandchild.

Aunt Sally raised her voice to gain everyone's attention and everybody quieted down. She wanted to set up a picnic for next year without the bother that this one had been of phone calls and coordinating everyone.

A hush fell over the area and everyone's attention centered on Aunt Sally.

Aunt Ruth grabbed my elbow and drew me closer. She said she'd never seen two people change as much as my sister and I had changed after high school.

So she had noticed that too! Huh… The thought gave me pause.

Aunt Sally started to talk about preparations for next year.

I felt torn in two directions. Aunt Sally wanted me to pay attention, but Aunt Ruth tugged at my elbow.

I smiled and tried to be polite to Aunt Ruth. Aunt Ruth couldn't hear well anymore.

Aunt Ruth asked, "How'd you do it?"

Despite the intrusion, Aunt Sally carried on, "What about meeting next year at this same spot? What date should we make it?"

How had I done what… change? I pondered the question.

Over the years I'd given my grandmother's comment a lot of thought. During my twenties I hadn't understood what she meant at all.

Change, what change? As far as I could tell, I hadn't changed at all.

In my thirties I'd started to suspect that I had changed, but how? I couldn't identify how. When I looked back at my life then, all I saw was a seamless transition from childhood to adulthood.

But as decades passed, I gradually grasped what my grandmother had recognized instinctively.

I whispered to Aunt Ruth that I'd been dissatisfied with my lot growing up and that whenever I thought I could predict what my life was going to be like in five or ten years, I'd always begun doing something new right away, something that, if I succeeded, would guarantee that my life would have different scenery, would take a different trajectory, take me somewhere new and unpredictable.

"It's a bit like swimming," I said, warming to the subject.

"A bit like wh-a-t?"

I raised my voice so that Aunt Ruth could hear, "Swimming, which I finally learned how to do this year, by the way." I grinned. "I learned to just relax, focus on pulling in the next breath to support the next stroke. I became willing to lay the heaviest weight, my head, in the water and let my breath lift me up. I quit trying so hard."

Aunt Ruth said, "What did you say? I didn't hear."

"Learning to swim has guaranteed that I see life from the center of the pool instead of feeling like I'm stranded on shore. Whenever I do something new I become a different person. As a kid I always kept trying too hard to do something new. That's what made me appear to change so much."

Across the room, Aunt Sally's expression darkened. Her face hardened, resembling the thunder cloud I recalled seeing cross her face when her kids rioted through her living room. Steam was building in her stack.

Aunt Ruth persisted, "I don't understand. What do you mean?"

I said, "Well, it's like this, I—"

"Marilyn, SHUT UP!"

Now you probably think that when Aunt Sally yelled at me, I felt embarrassed. After all, an elderly woman, heading up a gathering of more than a hundred people, my entire extended family, singled me out to be quiet. All the ingredients for humiliation, right?

Instead a wave of joy enveloped me. I felt thrilled. She yelled at me exactly as if I was one of her kids! Aunt Sally had never done that before. I was included!

As a child I'd thought I had to put out extra effort or I'd never be accepted. It was no fun having to behave for all of those adults, every one of whom set a different standard that I couldn't hope to discover and meet in time to please. Like a dumb ass, I never considered pleasing myself.

And here was Aunt Sally, with one bellow, leveling all of creation with her frustration and including me as part of the realm she ruled.

I grinned. I was just as bad as any one of her wonderful kids!

Thanks to Aunt Sally, that day I discovered that it's never too late to realize that you, like Dorothy from the Wizard of Oz, are already exactly where you belong.

Author's Note

Writing helps me understand the who, what, how and why of living and see connections. This story was first written in 2013, the same year that my aunt yelled at me, which turned out to be the last time I saw her alive. I think it's interesting that this story found a publisher just after her death in 2017.

MRS. HAVERMILL ISN'T AS FAST AS SHE USED TO BE

by Peter Barlow

Morning comes too early for her tastes. She feels as if she hasn't slept at all, as if her eyes only just closed one moment and the next they're open again, but it's nine hours later. She doesn't feel refreshed, doesn't think she has dreamed, or if she has she can't remember any of them. If she stops to think—but that doesn't happen. There's far too much in her head, things from when she was a little girl all the way up to yesterday, and if she stops to think about anything then who knows where her mind will end up. She doesn't know. But she awakes hopeful that today will be a good day, a special day, with a minimum of family-based drama. That would be the best gift of all. Christmas, she finds, has become much more contentious than it used to be.

Rising is an issue. It takes a lot longer than it used to. Everything aches. Sleep doesn't make it any better. She can no longer stand up perfectly straight, the osteoporosis is so bad, and when it rains, every joint in her body seizes up from the arthritis. She hardly has any original parts anymore. Both knees, both hips, and an ankle have been replaced. There's a plate in her left wrist put there winter before last after she slipped on the ice on her front walk going after the mail, breaking her wrist. But a long rise time is built into her morning routine. She sits and then stands carefully. It would be a fine day, she thinks, if she were to fall and break a rib.

She starts toward the kitchen. The trip from her bedside to the counter where the coffee pot sits is about forty feet and takes her down a short hallway and through her living room. It takes her a little less than two minutes to make the trip. She knows this, knows she used to be faster, but she doesn't care. Most of her days are wide open, so there isn't a point in rushing. She programs the coffee pot the night before, so by the time she gets there it's already brewed. She pours herself a mug and goes back into the living room, to her favorite comfy chair, another minute on her feet. She sets the mug on the small table next to the chair, and she reclines slightly and turns the television on. She has only just made herself comfortable when the phone rings. It's a few seconds after she picks up before the synapses fire enough for her to say, "Hello."

Her son is on the other end. Glenn Junior. She hadn't wanted to call him that, had wanted to give him his own name, his own identity, but her husband vetoed that. Glenn is a good name, he'd said, a solid name, my name, don't you think my name is solid, Eileen, don't you think I'm solid? Glenn Junior turned out to be something less than solid as the day is long. He almost never called her himself. Usually he made his wife do it. Hearing him on the phone now made her happy, though. You're still coming today, aren't you dear? she says, I've already started on lunch. He is still coming. She didn't have to start on lunch, he says. He and Lexy and the kids are bringing the ham and a few sides and a salad; she shouldn't trouble herself. If you're sure, dear, she says. He's sure. She wonders if he knows she hasn't started anything yet. Best not to tell him. Might make him angry, and with his temper—best to play this game this way. They say their goodbyes and hang up, and she tries to remember where her coffee is.

A time passes—she doesn't know quite how long—this is what she has noticed about retirement: time is more abstract now. She knows of fellow retirees whose days are filled. Some have returned to work. Some have occupied themselves with long-unfulfilled projects of fancy, building birdhouses, learning to dance. That is not her. When she went back to work after Glenn Junior was old enough to mind himself and Glenn Senior was gone, she worked hard. Her work, excepting her son, was her life. When the work ended, she told herself while she was working, she would relax. Read. Garden. Fill her hours with quiet contemplation and the occasional visit from her son and his family. This is what she has done, and the hours of the day don't mean what they once did.

Vacuum, she thinks. Wipe the counters, she thinks. Tidy, she thinks. That was supposed to be next. She stands up and goes to the closet where the cleaning materials are. In the minute and a half it takes her to get there, she thinks: It will be good to see them all again. What a darling Lexy is, and so good for him. They look after each other well. That's what a good marriage is: two people who look after each other well. And she's certainly done her part, more than. And Glenn, Glenn is probably half a head taller than he was the last time I saw him. He takes after his father like that. I just wish he wasn't picking up all of the character traits as well. And little Molly is just the most darling little girl. Polite, too. Says please and thank you and Mother may I. She'll be a heartbreaker when she's—wait. Where am I? What was I doing? I'm in front of the storage closet—oh, right. Cleaning. Let's see...

Eileen gets the vacuum out and plugs it in. This is not without its difficulties. Anything between waist- and shoulder-level is not an issue, but lower things like power outlets are problematic. She doesn't bend too well. Her back is largely inflexible, and bending at the knees not an easy task. The doctors assured her when they were preparing her for surgery that she would notice a marked improvement in her mobility afterwards. She completed all of her physical therapy dutifully. Lexy, bless her, took some time off of work to shuttle her back and forth. (Glenn Junior declined to help, even though he had more vacation time built up and his job pays slightly less than Lexy's. Eileen remembers hearing one side of an argument on the topic via an overheard phone call.) But the advertised marked improvement never came. She could walk and bend much the same as she had before, but no better. The vacuum, though, affords her something to lean against, something to help take the pressure off her back and knees and hips and ankles.

Rarely does clean-up take less than an hour. Everything is thoroughly cleaned. The vacuum stays at one point for two or three seconds at a stretch, giving it more time to pull dirt and whatnot from the shag carpet. With so little dirt accumulating between cleanings, however, it's difficult to the untrained eye to tell what's just been cleaned. She knows, though. She can tell. She doesn't miss a square inch of exposed carpet either. The counters in the kitchen are handled in much the same fashion, each swipe of the sponge taking several seconds to get from one side to the other, every portion of the counter receiving some cleaner. Glenn Junior has said a few times that her counters are clean enough to eat off of, though he's never tried to do that himself. *Perhaps today*, she thinks, but she knows better. When she's finished, the counters are the pristine white of tofu.

Making herself ready comes next. This part she takes seriously, and the time she spends doing it, she considers well spent. The shower has a removable hand-held head; Glenn Junior had it installed around the time of her first hip replacement, when the family was told standing in the shower for her would be a chore. There's a bench seat in there as well, and all of her extra needs—soap and shampoo and such—are at arm level. Her shower today, as it has for as long as she can remember, takes fifteen minutes. It would be shorter but she shampoos her hair twice, deliberately. She is proud of her hair, in no small part because it has not grayed, and she fears that if she cared for it less it would be. No one has bothered to tell her otherwise.

In the bedroom afterwards, she dresses—a simple floral-print dress that stops somewhere mid-shin, the way her father would approve of—and does her make-up. She has a proper vanity in one corner of her bedroom, and a stool that is more comfortable than it looks. Glenn Senior made them both himself—he made most of the wood furnishings in the home—but the original stool had no padding on it, something Glenn Junior, or more specifically Lexy, corrected at the same time the bench seat and removable shower head were put in. All these years later the seat has not lost its plump. Granted, enough padding was installed that it was going to be comfortable for a good long while anyway, but it hasn't shown any signs of breaking down yet, and because of that the vanity stool has become one of her favorite places in the house. Mrs. Havermill only weighs ninety pounds soaking wet; when she sits on the stool, it doesn't even sigh.

Layering of make-up is not something she does. She doesn't think she needs to. All her life she's been told she's pretty, and while she doesn't completely agree—she's much too modest for that—she doesn't think she needs to pile make-up on her face to look good or even passable. Her skin is clear, something she attributes to a reasonably healthy diet and the lack of any harmful vices. A light blush and maybe some eyeliner is all she does. She doesn't like seeing women who are basically all make-up. The last time she was at the senior center she saw a couple of women who were a base of white away from looking like clowns.

Later, when everyone has left, she will reflect on this morning, on its quiet, its calm, and think how nice it was. She has forgotten that this morning is, in every respect except for the phone call and impending family visit, identical to the morning of the day before, and the day before that, and the day before that. Those days, as this one, she had her coffee, she vacuumed, she showered, dressed, and sat at her vanity. Last evening, and the evenings before that, she reflected on the morning, the quiet, the calm, and thought how nice it was. This happens every day. She is unaware of this.

*

In what seems like no time, Glenn Junior and his family are there. It seems like no time because it was. The process of showering, dressing, and making herself up takes two hours total, including the commute time. She was only in her comfy chair for five minutes when the door opened. They let themselves in; Glenn Junior has had a key since Glenn Senior passed away, and he is well aware that if he were to knock and wait it would be upwards of five minutes before she answers the door. In summer they wouldn't mind so much, but it's Christmas Day, fifteen degrees out and six inches of snow on the ground, so entering unannounced—which she's used to anyway—causes no drama.

She smiles as the children come through first, shouting "Grandma! Grandma!" as they run toward her. Glenn Glenn jumps on her lap and hugs her so tight she may burst, while Molly grabs her arm from where it sits on the armrest and squeezes like a human blood pressure machine. Lexy is through next, covered casserole in hands, and she scolds the children gently, "Now, now, children, not so rough on her, she's not so strong, you know." Mrs. Havermill sees Glenn Junior nod from the doorway and disappear back outside, probably going after more food. Glenn Glenn has started rattling off what Santa brought him for Christmas in that breathless way that eight-year-olds do, fast enough that she can't keep up; she thinks she hears him say "toy train set" but she isn't sure. Molly is, as she usually is, drowned out by her older brother but she seems content just holding on to her grandmother's arm. The children are carrying no food, and in the rush of her grandson's words she struggles to remember why—ah, yes. At Thanksgiving, Glenn Glenn dropped the dish with the hot buttered corn in it. It took two times with a rented carpet shampoo machine to get all the butter out.

Now Glenn Junior comes back in, two dishes stacked one atop the other. Lexy heads back outside, and as Glenn Junior passes by he tells Glenn Glenn to get off his grandmother and come and help. The boy does with a promise of, "I'll be right back, Grandma," and is out the front door as fast as he came through it. Molly squeezes her arm a little harder and says a faint something that she doesn't quite catch. She smiles at the girl and tries to remember the last time she heard the girl's voice. Was it Thanksgiving? Over the summer holiday? This time last year? She can't recall. She pats Molly on the shoulder, guessing but not knowing that this little bit of emotional nourishment is more than she's gotten all day, thanks to Glenn Glenn, and is more than she usually receives.

The door opens again. The cold makes Molly shiver. She lets go of her grandmother and runs off toward the bedroom, probably to sit on the vanity stool. Glenn Glenn is carrying a vegetable platter with plastic wrap on. "Look, Grandma," he says on his way past her. Glenn Junior, carrying two more casseroles, closes the front door with a foot and stamps the snow from his boots. It's then she notices that Glenn Glenn didn't do the same, and tracked snow some three feet into the center of the living room. Glenn Junior grunts an apology as he goes by her and a second later the room is quiet again. All of the noise is contained in the kitchen, most of it coming from Glenn Glenn. She takes a moment to savor it. She loves her family, truly, but every now and again she thinks it'd be nicer if they—Glenn Glenn particularly—were at half volume. *Ah, well. The boy will grow out of it. He'll be sullen in no time. Glenn Junior was moody as all get out as a teenager, and Glenn Glenn is just showing off for Grandma.*

As soon as Glenn Glenn hits her lap again he's back to talking about his Christmas gifts, how cool they all are, what all of the special features are. He speaks so fast his words seem to blend together. There are syllables in his words somewhere, but where exactly is hard to say. Glenn Glenn speaks for a minute before Lexy re-enters the room and tells him to get off his grandmother and go and sit on the couch. He does with a sneer on his face that he thinks she doesn't notice, and no sooner does he get there than he complains about what's on the television. Mrs. Havermill turned it on in the few minutes between getting ready and their arrival, but can't honestly say she's given it any attention. It came on to a wildlife special, Tigers of the African Veldt, which is still playing. Apparently it doesn't meet Glenn Glenn's approval because nobody's dying or getting cut up and no athletes are involved. What he doesn't know is that two minutes after the channel is changed, which will happen shortly, graphic footage of an adult male tiger attacking and killing a male cub will be shown. Had he seen it, Glenn Glenn would have been amazed, but with his complaining Mrs. Havermill is considering shutting the thing off.

Sitting next to her son, Lexy tells Glenn Glenn to be quiet again. He does, and the next thing said comes from the television: "The tigress bears three cubs, two females and a male." Mrs. Havermill is lost in thought for a moment. She and Glenn had but one child, Glenn Junior, and lost two others in utero, both girls. She thinks from time to time how things would have been different had those children survived.

How would they have been treated? Would I have raised them well? More people for the holidays, anyway, and somewhere in the middle of that thought she realizes that Lexy has asked her something. Mrs. Havermill mutters an apology. "I said, how are you feeling today?" Oh, pretty good, hips are feeling much better today but the knees still don't like the cold. "Have you thought any more about what we talked about at Thanksgiving? The people at the facility are really good. They can help you manage your pain a little better." She's heard this before. She's not in much pain, she says, which is more or less true; the problem is not pain, the problem is age, and no doctor can reverse that. Besides, my Glenn wouldn't like it if I left this house, she says.

Further discussion is lost to the sudden appearance and accompanying blare of football on the television. Glenn Junior is in the other recliner—how did that happen? He isn't known for his stealth—and has the remote control in his hands. Both women look at him while Glenn Glenn cheers at the sight of twenty-two heavily-padded college students running into each other, not knowing or caring much who the teams are. Lexy sighs; she's not much into sports. Mrs. Havermill just looks at him, at the way he is sitting in the chair, his posture, how his arms sit on the armrests, the slightly cocked way he holds the can of beer he's drinking. She sees this and thinks, *That's my Glenn, every bit of him, identical down to the DNA.*

A moment later, Molly reenters the room. Her grandmother is the only one to notice this, and that only because she was looking in the general direction of the kitchen. Molly is carrying a small glass of orange juice, which she sips from as she takes a seat on the floor in front of her grandmother, so close that the older woman can braid the child's hair. Glenn Glenn is the next one to notice the glass of juice, although he doesn't do that until the next commercial break five minutes later. In the interim, Molly sits quietly, sipping, pretending to pay attention to the game but more focused on a wicker basket halfway between her and the television. The basket contains an array of magazines, National Geographic, Better Homes and Gardens, Good Housekeeping, none of which the five-year-old can understand or truly appreciate but all of which hold more intrigue to her than the twenty-two heavily-padded college students running into each other on the television. Mrs. Havermill knows the girl wants to pick up one of the magazines and flip through it. She also knows what will happen after that: Glenn Junior will tell Molly to leave the magazines alone, Glenn Glenn will make a snide comment and go after the juice, Molly will run for cover, probably into the bedroom, and Lexy will sit passively watching this happen. Knowing this, she is silently wishing Molly would just reach for a magazine, partly to just get the scene over with—it would happen at some point anyway—and partly because it would amuse her more than the football game, which doesn't.

Someone on the field calls time out, the network cuts to commercial, and Molly reaches for the basket. She pulls out the magazine on top, the previous month's National Geographic, sits back in front of her grandmother, and flips the magazine open. "Dad," Glenn Glenn says, "Molly's gotten into the magazines again. And she's got some juice." The boy leans forward but he's moved less than six inches when Lexy puts an arm in front of him. He stops, casts a glance at his mother that is distinctly lacking in fear, and sits back into the sofa. "That's not fair," he says. "Molly gets away with everything because she's a girl." Molly has paid none of this any attention, engrossed instead by an article about the bald eagle. Her grandmother watches all of this intently, marveling at how much she misread the situation.

The oven timer goes off just then. "Let's eat," Glenn Junior says, and stands up. Glenn Glenn bounces off the sofa and runs into the dining room before anyone else can even get up. Lexy scurries after her son, Molly close behind. Mrs. Havermill struggles to rise from her comfy chair; by the time she does, Glenn Junior has already gone into the dining room too. She is alone. This doesn't surprise her. She starts the commute to the kitchen and gets maybe a third of the way there when Lexy reappears. Glenn Junior has taken over the ham carving duties, and she has come to help Mrs. Havermill. Lexy takes her by the arm and elbow. Better balanced and supported, she can move quicker. When she is seated thirty seconds later, Glenn Junior has already started eating and Glenn Glenn is serving himself. Molly is sitting patiently. Mrs. Havermill frowns and sits at the head of the table. She doesn't like sitting there— that spot was Glenn's.

As the meal progresses, three things becomes more evident: one, that Glenn Junior's iron-fisted control over his family is still in place; two, that Glenn Glenn, following his father's example, has quashed Molly's spirit to the point where the girl is afraid to do anything at all; and three,

Lexy knows both of these things. The second point is illustrated almost as soon as grace is over. Molly and Glenn Glenn are seated next to each other, opposite their mother. Near the center of the table is a basket of rolls. Molly takes one and puts it on her plate but as she's reaching for the butter Glenn Glenn takes the roll, licks it, and puts it back with a laugh. Molly starts crying. Glenn Junior slams his knife down. "You will not cry at the dinner table, young lady. Or would you like to be disciplined again?" Glenn Glenn laughs longer. Lexy throws Glenn Junior a scowl. He looks in her direction with a challenging sneer and returns to his turkey. Mrs. Havermill frowns and says nothing, and wonders how Molly manages to eat anything aside from what the boy doesn't like, like broccoli.

She will reflect on all of this again later, when they're gone, with some sadness. What she doesn't know, can't possibly know, is that Molly will eventually be a senator. Glenn Glenn will not finish high school, and will struggle to support himself as an adult. Had she known this then, she would have smiled. At the moment she says nothing, and swallows a pill.

*

Soon, the meal is done. Molly manages to eat something, timing her bites to her brother's so that he would be occupied. Lexy's scowl, while it lightened slightly, does not entirely go away. Neither Glenn Junior nor Glenn Glenn says anything else. Glenn Junior leaves the table as soon as he finishes and goes back into the living room to watch the football. Glenn Glenn follows suit a minute later. Mrs. Havermill is barely halfway through her plate. Molly starts eating more then, but Mrs. Havermill can see clearly now the puffiness around the girl's eyes. *She must cry a lot,* Mrs. Havermill thinks. *Poor girl.*

"How would it be," Lexy says then, "if I left? Just walked out. Took Molly, packed up our troubles, and left. He's your son, I know, but he's just—terrible. I don't recognize him anymore. And he lets Glenn Glenn get away with anything. Won't discipline him at all. Won't hear of it. Doesn't defend Molly. Doesn't let me defend her. And I—think I've had enough. I really do. The kind, generous man I married is just—gone now, and I—I—"

Eileen thinks for a moment, about what Lexy is saying, about whether or not Glenn Junior had always been that way. She hadn't disciplined him much growing up either, she knows this. A lot of it she had written off to boys being boys but—was it really? Glenn never did any disciplining. Usually he just laughed whenever Glenn Junior did anything wrong, wrote off his bad grades to hyperactivity, something that was perfectly normal and to be expected. When any punishments needed to be handed out, though, he wasn't around, and when he was he countermanded anything Eileen did. She thinks about this for a long moment, then she puts her hand on top of Lexy's, and tries to fill her with calm.

"Use the back door. I'll send out Molly." She squeezes. A tear goes down Lexy's face. "Go. Out the back door."

She gives Lexy a hug—a slight one; she isn't all that strong—and goes back into the living room. Glenn Glenn has taken her comfy chair. Molly has the sofa to herself. Glenn Junior is back in the recliner he had been in earlier. She sits down next to Molly and whispers into her ear to go into the kitchen, quickly. Molly jumps up and runs into the next room. Mrs. Havermill rises, goes over in front of her comfy chair, and stands there in front of it. Glenn Glenn tilts to one side and then the other. "Jeez, Grandma, you're blocking the view of the television." She doesn't move, looking down on him and frowning a little. "What? You move your feet, you lose your seat. Everybody knows that." Her frown grows slightly. "Dad, I think Grandma's having an issue or something. She won't move."

Eileen smiles as the sound of a motor starting came from outside. Glenn Junior sat up quickly. "What the hell?" He scans the room and a look of shock comes onto his face. "Lexy?" He runs to the front door and flings it open. "Goddammit!" Glenn Glenn stands up and squeezes around his grandmother to get to the front door. She sits down in her comfy chair, picks up the remote, and changes the channel back to the wildlife program. From outside the cursing grows fainter and fainter; she guesses Glenn Junior was chasing after the minivan. A couple of minutes later he comes back inside, breathing hard, his face red from the cold and the exertion, holding an icicle in his hand like a shiv.

"Do you know anything about this?" he says to Glenn Glenn. The boy shakes his head and backs away from his father, a frightened look on his face. "What about you?" he says to his mother. "Do you know what this is about?" She smiles. Glenn Junior kneels down in front of her. "I said," he says, his mouth barely opening, "do you know what this is about?" She keeps smiling. She saw this anger in him as a child and caved. Now, she wasn't going to. He grabs her by the arms. "Do you think this is funny?" Out of the corner of her eye, she sees Glenn Glenn scamper to the nearest thing to higher ground he can find: the sofa.

"This *is* funny." The smile, if anything, widens. "And sad. I thought I raised you better than this. Turns out I didn't. You have no idea how disappointing that is." Glenn Junior lets go of her then and storms out the front door. Glenn Glenn still has the terrified look on his face. "You should catch up to him." The boy was gone a moment later. She stands up and walks to the door. By the time she gets there, they are out of sight. She closes it, and the sound of the latch catching is the most satisfying sound she's heard since her youth.

One day later, a delivery man shows up at Mrs. Havermill's front door with a bouquet of flowers. The card reads: "Thank you, thank you, thank you. We'll be in touch as soon as we're safe. Lexy and Molly." In time, Lexy will remarry and Molly comes to regard her new stepfather as more of a father than her real one. They only see Glenn Junior once more in their lives, at a child support hearing held before Lexy remarried. He glowers at the pair of them but neither one cares.

But that day, after everyone is gone, Mrs. Havermill does little else. She sits in front of the television and learns more about the Tigers of the African Veldt, about how they were dying out due to encroachment by humans onto their land and climate change shrinking the space where food could be found. She feels sad about this too, because tigers deserve better. Everyone deserves better. But she is no help in their survival, nor they hers, so she does nothing but mourn for a moment and then consider—

Eileen Havermill never gets that far. It is ten days before she is discovered. The mailbox gets full to overflowing and the mailman, meaning well, comes to her front door to see if there was a note or anything. It opens when he knocks, and both the sight and smell of her makes him gag. What was unmistakable, though, was the smile on her face, happy, inviting, warm.

Author's Note

I'd had this character, this old lady who couldn't hardly move at all, bopping around my head for a long time. It took me a few tries spread over a decade or so until I figured out what her story really was. Because it's really a simple story if you think about it, and because I can't leave well enough alone, I dressed it up and made it a double acrostic as a bit of a bonus.

DELICIOUS TENSION:

An Interview with Daniel Simpson

Daniel Simpson and his identical twin brother, David, were born blind in Williamsport, Pennsylvania, in 1952. After attending the Overbrook School for the Blind through eighth grade (1956–1966), Dan became one of the first blind students in his county to go to a public school. He earned a Bachelor of Arts in English and music from Muhlenberg College, Allentown, Pennsylvania, where he graduated Summa cum Laude and Class Salutatorian. After receiving a Master of Music degree in organ performance from Westminster Choir College, Princeton, New Jersey, where he had the opportunity to sing with major symphony orchestras, Dan traveled to Paris for a year of private study with the world-renowned blind organist André Marchal. Since then, Dan has worked as a church musician, computer programmer, and high school English teacher, earning a Master of Arts in English and a teaching certificate from the University of Pennsylvania along the way.

In 2014, Poets Wear Prada published *School for the Blind,* his debut collection of poems. This year, he and his wife, Ona Gritz, collaborated as co-authors of *Border Songs: A Conversation in Poems* (Finishing Line Press) and as co-editors of *More Challenges for the Delusional: Peter Murphy's Prompts and the Writing They Inspired*, forthcoming from Diode Editions. His work has appeared in *Prairie Schooner, The Cortland Review, HampdenSydney Poetry Review, Passager, Schuylkill Valley Journal, The Atlanta Review, The Louisville Review, Margie,* and *The New York Times*, among other publications. In 2007, he and his brother released a CD of their poetry entitled *Audio Chapbook*. Cinquo Puntos Press published his essay "Line Breaks the Way I See Them" and four of his poems in *Beauty Is A Verb: The New Poetry of Disability*, a 2012 ALA Notable Poetry Book called "unusual and powerful" by Publisher's Weekly in a starred review.

Mark Danowsky: Reading your poem "Dolly" I'm particularly struck by the line, "Let them mail out all your desire." There's often something startling about your delivery; I'd like to hear a few words about your approach to lineation.

Daniel Simpson: I actually wrote a fairly detailed essay called "Line Breaks The Way I See Them," which appeared in the anthology *Beauty Is a Verb: The New Poetry of Disability* and in the online journal *Wordgathering*.

At the center of it was a discussion I had with the poet Molly Peacock when I first sought her out to serve as a mentor. She asked this same question you are posing. At that time, even though I am blind, I paid attention to the appearance of a poem on the page, more or less neatening up lines so the right margin stayed fairly even. I knew from working with previous teachers and receiving feedback from other poets that many believed that doing so increased the aesthetics of the poem.

"Having lines of relatively the same length can make a poem look beautiful on the page," Molly said, "but that's a painterly thing to do. Why do you care how it looks on the page? You're blind, and that seems like a particularly sighted concern. Besides that, you're a musician. Wouldn't it make more sense in the context of your life to treat the poem and its line breaks more like a musical score than a painting? For now, at least for your next couple of poems, why not try this? Don't worry about making the poem look pretty on the page. Just listen to your natural cadence and let the line breaks act as indicators in a musical score as to where you want the performers to breathe or to place more emphasis. And if one line sticks way out like a big shirt billowing on a clothesline, and the next line hangs like a limp little sock next to it, so be it. What do you care?"

She had a point. For a while, I tried it. It stretched my thinking about the line and gave me some practical idea of what Charles Olson must have been talking about in his discussions of line length and the breath. Eventually, though, I moderated lines so they didn't have the extreme differences in length that early experiments did, but I never went back to worrying about evenness.

Even though I now write mostly in free verse, I feel a pull toward four or five beats per line. In "Dolly," however, I see that lines can vary from two to five beats and are mostly end-stopped. When I'm writing down a poem, I just let an almost unconscious sense of rhythm guide me. Analyzing too much at that point takes me out of the poem. But I try to guard against a leaning toward so many end-stop lines now, since thinking a little about where to break a line can create a delicious tension. So, for example, if I see a place where holding a word back until the beginning of the next line will give it more weight or a double entendre, I'll do it.

MD: Thinking about your poem "What To Do When," what can poetry offer when we're grieving?

DS: Poetry, like memoir, can provide a contradiction to the isolation we can feel, especially during grief. Poetry says, "This is what it's like for me. What is it like for you?" It has the added advantages of concision and attention to the music of language. In ordinary times, many people dream of writing the "great American novel," but watch how many turn to poetry in times of national crisis such as 9/11. When we're grieving, we look for something we can hold on to, and poems provide that.

MD: What is the role of writing in your daily routine?

DS: When I'm at my best, writing plays a primary role in my daily routine. I work best in the morning, that wonderful time when the subconscious hasn't slipped completely from view and my sense of energy and possibility is at its apex. I aim to be at my desk around 8:30. Fortunately, I have two dogs who love breakfast as much as I do, so they keep me honest—sometimes more than necessary—when it comes to getting out of bed. Partly due to good fortune and partly due to effort on my part, I have managed to set up my life so that my paid work comes later in the day, allowing me the luxury of writing when I'm at my best.

I saw a remark from Joan Didion that expresses well my primary reasons for writing: "I write entirely to find out what I'm thinking, what I'm looking at, what I see and what it means. What I want and what I fear."

Of course, when I go to the desk, I always hope that, ultimately, I'm making something meaningful that will last and will speak to someone else. Needless to say, that doesn't always happen, which is why I have to keep those primary reasons in focus to sustain me through those days when nothing much happens. Writing centers me. If I go for several days without writing, I feel less grounded.

MD: Do you have any writing-related habits?

DS: Besides trying to keep a regular schedule, I allow myself to read for up to an hour before I start writing. I don't make this a hard and fast rule; if I feel a strong pull to get down to writing immediately, I go with it. (Never say no to the muse.) If I give into my curiosity and listen to the news during breakfast, I limit myself to 15 minutes. After all, "the world is too much with us, late and soon," especially during distressing times like ours. I need to experiment with resisting the urge to check the news before I write but, at any rate, I know not to let too much of the world crowd in on me before I try to write. Music sustains me, so I often immerse myself in music before I get to work. Good lyrics inspire me, and then there's the way that music itself can trigger lots of emotions and affect one's mood.

I find it helpful not to check email or answer the phone until I've finished my writing time, although I do allow myself about 10 minutes to organize my list of priorities for the day before I start reading and writing. I know this sounds contradictory to keeping the world at bay, but for some reason, organizing a short list of things to accomplish that day makes it more possible to put those things aside, knowing that I have written them down and don't have to worry about forgetting something important to take care of later.

MD: What are the most enjoyable aspects of the writing process for you?

DS: I like best that space between the blank page and revising. You've gotten down a line or two, so you're beyond that land of nothingness, but all the surprises and possibilities of a brand new poem still await you. My brother Dave once interviewed the poet Marie Howe for a podcast. In it, she talked about her process. "I'll just write and write and write and write and write and write and write," she said, "until something catches. I'll just start writing into that other key, if you know what I mean. It takes me a long time to get there, so I write a lot. And then, something happens. You start being dragged along by something else. The horse, if you will, starts riding you, and that is the greatest feeling in the world because then all you have to do is hold tight, hold onto the reins and trust that the horse knows where it's going. I guess that horse would be Pegasus." Who doesn't love that moment when the horse starts riding you? I do revise a lot and generally over a long time, maybe even years, and am learning to enjoy that process more. But there's still nothing that matches that thrill when something outside of you seems to be running the show.

MD: What is the spark that begins a poem?

DS: Sometimes, they come as half-formed ideas. If I stop to analyze them, I think many of the sparks come as something even more vague— intimations, questions, curiosities. It's easier to identify their sources than to define them. Looking back at my poems, I see that their sparks came from all over, as I suspect most writers' do. Here is just a partial list:

> Bible stories and other classic literature
> an infestation of squirrels in my house
> writing prompts
> setting out to write in a poetic form
> freewriting
> snippets of conversation, overheard or otherwise
> news stories
> an interview with Joseph Campbell
> events, large and small, from childhood
> small intimacies and awkward moments in relationships
> major events in my more recent life that needed sorting out

MD: When do you decide a poem is complete? Is this related to a sense of satisfaction or closure?

DS: In principle, I agree with the statement attributed to Paul Valery: "A poem is never finished, only abandoned." I say, "in principle" because I have some poems I've lived with long enough without wanting to change them that, if some urge to tinker with them came along, I wouldn't trust it. I think that's the advantage of taking your time before putting your poems out in public. My approach to publishing poems isn't unlike my approach to decision making. I tend to agonize for a long time, but once I come to a conclusion, I tend not to waver about it. Still, you never know. I've had the experience of reading some of my own poems after they have remained unchanged for a long time, even after they have been published, and hearing something new. I've even republished them in their altered form.

Overall, however, I do think you have to be satisfied with a poem before you publish it. You have to come to at least enough of a sense of closure that you believe (1) that you've taken it as far as you think you can and (2) it's good. Even if you allow that a poem might not be quite perfect, you make an assessment about diminishing returns. Essentially, you make a choice about how you want to spend your time and creative energy. You have to ask yourself, "Is it worth continuing to work on this poem which hasn't changed in a long time, or would I be better served by turning that attention toward creating new poems?"

You have to ask the same question about poems you have lived with for a while, which haven't changed, and which don't satisfy you. Anyone who knows me well knows I have a hard time getting rid of anything I think I might need or want later. It's even harder with poems. Even the ones that don't quite work still have a place in my heart; we've put in a lot of time together and I've gotten attached to them. Fortunately, Molly Peacock helped me ease the pain of shelving failed poems. "Make two piles," she said, "a Yes pile and a Maybe pile. The Yes poems get to go out for dinner, and the Maybe poems are just going to stay at home for a nice lunch."

MD: Do you share your poems with others prior to seeking publication?

DS: Yes. Back when I had a long-term working relationship with a teacher or mentor, that was the point. Now, I still occasionally take poems to workshops led by poets I admire, but I've also learned to take comments, particularly from the other participants, with a grain of salt. If everybody loves a particular line or image, that's usually a good sign. If nobody understands a certain line, you'd better think again about it. But if opinion is divided, you haven't learned a lot unless somebody can articulate more convincingly than others why something works or doesn't and, if it doesn't, how you might fix the problem.

Mostly, I limit myself to a few trusted readers, people who know me and what I'm trying to do and who aren't trying to make me write like them. Ona, my wife, who is also a poet and writer, comes first. I used to count on my brother Dave, too, before he died. Even while he was sick, I could run a poem by him, and he'd have something valuable to say. I also have a friend, the poet and essayist Molly Fisk, who reads me well and gives feedback in a way that feels expansive rather than restrictive. I like a critic who has some distance from the poem, yet feels like they're in my corner.

One important thing I've learned over the years is to be clear about what I want from a reader. Sometimes, I just feel so pleased that I've gotten something down that I want to read it to someone. In those situations, I've learned to say, "I just want to share this day's accomplishment with you and see what it feels like to read it out loud to someone. I'm not ready yet for someone else's take on it." It's important to me to find my own way for a while with a poem. Later, I can say that I'm ready for reactions and suggestions.

MD: How has your vision of success as a poet shifted over the course of your writing life?

DS: It's more internal and less external in its focus. To put it more starkly, it's more about doing the work today and less about immortality. I used to gloss over my successes and dwell too much on my failures and on making comparisons with others. I'm not immune to those things now. It's just that those negative things are quieter. Of course, one reason they're quieter, ironically, is that I've accomplished an important, product-oriented goal: I have books I can hold in my hand that are mine—books I'm proud of. That doesn't mean I don't still hear rumblings within about more books and greater recognition. But I'm better at turning away from them and thinking about the work at hand and how much I love the processes of reading, thinking, keeping my heart open, and writing. In these times, anything we do to keep the poetic and the creative alive in us and in the world counts as a success. "Just do the work," I tell myself, "and let the externals take care of themselves."

MD: Who do you write for? Has your target audience changed?

DS: While I'm writing a poem, I'm mostly interested in my relationship with that poem, where my mind and that poem are taking me. In the background, I suppose I hope that someone will want to read that poem and get something from it someday, but I don't feel like I'm writing directly to them. I think that's been fairly constant over time.

MD: Who do you enjoy reading these days?

DS: Most recently, I've been reading Mary Oliver and Charles Bukowski. Mary Oliver is one of my mainstays. Probably like many, I feel a kinship with her sensibility, although I would never call myself a "nature poet." Yet, when I read her, I think, "Oh yes, I want to have that kind of attention for the world and the goings-on of life." I got interested in Charles Bukowski precisely because his narrators challenge the smoothness and gentleness of mine. He's so raw and gritty and, sometimes, even vulgar. But one of the great things about poetry—any good literature, really—is that if the writer draws his characters well, you soon find yourself seeing a reflection of some part of yourself. Reading him is a long-term project, partially because *The Pleasures of the Damned: Poems, 1951-1993* is a large book and partially because I can't read him in large doses. That doesn't mean I don't enjoy reading him. Something about his voice can really grab me, and I want to know who he is and how he does what he does.

MD: Is there a poet whose work you never tire of reading?

DS: There are many. In fact, one definition of hell would be having to limit myself to one poet I love reading. Besides Mary Oliver, I'd list Stephen Dunn, Gregory Djanikian, Walt Whitman, Tony Hoagland, Robert Frost, Sharon Olds, Marie Howe, and John Donne.

MD: What advice do you have for poets/writers?

DS: Feel free to write shitty first drafts. Lock the internal editor out of the room while you're playing/experimenting/creating.

Don't settle for first drafts. Very rarely does everything come out just right on the first pass.

Read your work aloud when you're writing and revising. If you find yourself tripping over the same place every time, there's something that needs to be fixed. If you get a niggling feeling about the logic or content in some line, don't gloss over it.

Be patient with your work. Don't rush it into publication until it's ready. But once it's ready, make time to get it out into the world. (This is one of the harder parts for me of being a writer, so I'm giving this advice to myself as I'm giving it to you.)

Read widely. It will improve your writing immensely. Writing is just one half of the conversation.

Take time to figure out the right balance between asking others for their opinions of your work and coming to your own thinking about it.

Take it from Uncle Walt; loafing is good. As he wrote in "Song of Myself":

> "I loafe and invite my soul,
> I lean and loafe at my ease … observing a spear
>   of summer grass."

I know it's radical, but hide all clocks and cell phones, remove all other distractions, and dare yourself to drift toward boredom. What you find there might amaze you.

Keep your appointments with the writer in you. Even if the most you can figure out is fifteen minutes, three times a week, honor it. In my early days as a serious poet, I asked Mary Oliver about her writing process. She said, "Think of that writer within you as a shy person. Anyone who has tried to befriend a shy person knows that you have to keep showing up if you want her to feel safe enough to reveal herself. If you honor your appointments, she'll work between times on the writing problems you haven't yet solved and be ready with possible solutions when you return. But if you throw her over for a sale at Kmart, don't expect much when you finally show up."

MD: Is there anything on your mind, in general, that you'd like to share with readers?

DS: Earlier, I mentioned the poet Gregory Djanikian. If you don't know of him and his work, please read him. He's been a great model for me.

He doesn't blow his own horn; he just does the work. And what fabulous work it is—so full of heart and mind! He has a way of saying things that are at once completely fresh and inevitable. If I had to single out one poem to start with, it would be "The Journey," the same one that first hooked me. It's the first poem in his first book, *Man in the Middle*.

This leads into my second thought. I think we as poets can do more to champion the work of other poets. I've decided to include at least one poem by another poet in all the readings I give. Lately, I often read something by my brother, who isn't around anymore to read his own work. It can be a way of keeping someone's presence and work alive. But it doesn't have to be just that. In the music world, singers and bands cover other people's music all the time. Why shouldn't we poets do the equivalent thing for our comrades?

LISTENING TO NEW YORK RADIO
IN THE MIDDLE OF THE NIGHT

There, in insomniac City
where the dial can easily hold
five languages beyond English
and stations bleed into each other,
Emily Dickinson—satisfied
she could no longer see to see—
spoke through a piano
while a Spanish man, half-crying,
half singing, declared he too
would die if the one he most
desired did not give him
her undying love.
Between Emily and the Spanish man,
a sitar spoke harmoniously
about rock-steady faith,
while picking its way along
a path of dissonant doubt.
Commercial life finally
put to bed, Lennon
woke up from a good dream,
his imagination intact.
He sang with the sitar, calling
the chutney and raita left over
from last night's dinner to put on
spiritual livery.
They in turn inspired
the beans in my cabinet
to take on a holy presence,
and the cabinets themselves,
dazed at first, recalled
the distant spirits of trees.

And when the whole house became
tuned like this to the radio,
my father kindly caught
a coach from that other kingdom
to sit in my living room,
if only for a moment,
and casually talk with me
of ordinary life.

From *Border Songs: A Conversation in Poems* (Finishing Line Press, 2017), first appeared in *Nine Mile Magazine*.

MY PANTS ARE DRENCHED WITH RAIN

My pants are drenched with rain,
which came sideways and up my legs
as I walked home from the bus.

Once, Jenny filled my hand with hers
as we walked in the drizzle.
Her hands were wide and quiet—
hands that could listen,
quiet like a priest at confession.

My father's hands were busy,
not soft and uncaloused like mine.
I touched all the caskets before I chose
a pine box that was smooth and lean—
no nicks or splinters like the rocking boat
he hammered together for me in the cellar.
I picked a pine box and the sun poured down.

But now, my pants are drenched with rain.
May there be no time this weekend—
no time and not too much sun.
May there be no more train whistles
saying you must go somewhere,
and none of the usual loneliness.

I have other pants, dry pants,
that would match the red shirt with the swan,
the one I have on.

I am rich; my ears are full of talk.
Once, my arms were full of someone half my age.
Her shirt was filling up with water
and yet she breathed air in and out.
She did this repeatedly and without effort.
Everything she did amazed me.

Pretty soon, I will be dry.
Will the memory of my father fade
the way rain evaporates?

My mind is full of words.
I have not run out of things to say.
I make emphatic statements about the future and the present:
"Jesus shall reign" and "the rain it raineth every day."

How many years of rain
make dust of a wooden coffin?

One week after my father was buried,
it was raining, and I was touching myself,
thinking of Debbie, who wrote on our prom picture
that she would never forget the night we had.

Jenny just called to say
it is raining in Seattle now, too.
My mind is full of rain, and my heart of dust and longing.

From *Border Songs: A Conversation in Poems* (Finishing Line Press, 2017), first appeared in *Nine Mile Magazine.*

PLATONIC SEX

"What a depressing idea of love, to make it a relation between two people, whose monotony must be vanquished as required by adding extra people."

> —*Gilles Deleuze and Claire Parnet*
> A Thousand Plateaus: Capitalism and Schizophrenia

So this is intercourse—
you asking me with your eyes to say
yes, I'm game, I'm up for this
lifelong tapestry of ideas,

and I asking you by touch
to pick up yesterday's thread
when you said I just learned from Yeats
how crosses and roses work together,

then you asking me by phone
what I meant about the difference
between passion and romance,
the middle path and mediocrity,

and we asking each other,
sitting in your cold car past midnight,
living and dead stars crossing and rising
over the whirling earth, to say perhaps,

to say that, if yes,
we would seek the others,
we would place ourselves
in the path of meteors.

First appeared in *Nine Mile Magazine.*

A BLIND BOY'S FIRST GLIMPSE OF HEAVEN

I climbed the stepladder to Heaven when I was eight,
my father spotting me from behind.
I liked that he stayed below.
How else could I hear where the world was?

"You can move around, Son, but shuffle your feet,
in case there's a stray bale of hay to trip over,
and you don't want to walk off the edge."

God was in a meeting, I guess.
Anyway, I never saw Him.
What had He done to Lucifer?
And what did the Bible mean by "cast him out?"

Did God have a squad of angel goons up there
to blind-side him from the back and shove him off?
I wanted to jump, to see if I'd survive.

Fifty years later, Aunt Polly said,
"You better get ready, Dan, if you want God
to take you up to be with your Dad again,
and won't it be great to finally see his face?"

I don't know. I'm just getting to love
this world for what it is, a flawed place
with its subway platforms overlooking the third rail,
its hay lofts, open sewers and loading docks,
and all the strangers who've looked out for me,
letting me take their arms to walk with them.

I'm thinking, the next time I see Aunt Polly,
I'm going to tell her about my new vision.
"It's really going to be something," I'll say.
"In Heaven, you'll finally get to be blind."

From *School for the Blind* (Poets Wear Prada, 2014) and *Border Songs: A Conversation in Poems* (Finishing Line Press, 2017), first appeared in *Wordgathering*.

DOLLY

You think you should prepare yourself
for a good deed
you've been meaning to do for months
with a hammer and nails
you haven't bought yet.
But first, you have a suitcase of letters
it's time to send,
so you walk along Lender's Avenue,
turn right past the access road,
and let yourself into the copy center
that doubles as post office annex.

Rose or Jo-Ellen will handle the letters,
but it's Dolly you watch
in the rear left corner,
her face of a peasant
who has just set down
a bucket of blackberries
she'll bake in a pie.

She hasn't been waiting for you in particular.

She turns in her light cotton dress brimming over
with fresh cream, turns toward machines that splash wild ink
and thump a rhythm your headboard once knew.
Starch and tight shoes are not things she knows.

Let them mail out all your desire
and see if they'll keep your suitcase
behind the counter until the day you return.
Then go from here to the abandoned cathedral
and walk alone the Stations of the Cross.
Feel how dry your mouth has become.
Try not to think about blackberry pie.

LIVING WITH OTHERS

Last night as I was leaving,
Animal Control was just arriving
to collect the squirrel from the baited trap.
Eight now in two weeks.

While I'm sleeping, showering, listening to Brahms,
they're up there gnawing, chasing, crying
in what sounds like sexy pleasure.
I don't know where they're coming in,
or how they're getting out.

I had a wife once, and some days
she chewed her way through my exterior.
On others, I flung the door wide open.

Maybe I should just return the cage,
learn to live with rodents
who, after all, only want to do
the things we say we honor:
make a stable home, raise their young.

But this is all wrong;
ex-wives and squirrels are not the same.
Still, last time, the wires that got crossed,
the burning,
the length of silence afterward.

WHAT TO DO WHEN

The sun shines for you.

Though I know this to be true,
when would it make sense, in your grief, to say that to you?
If not while your mother lies dying,
then when? After one year? Two?

How long after my lover walks off with half
my books and dinner plates, should you let me sip on a carafe
of sorrow before you burst in on me
with a story you hope will make me laugh?

Every Sunday, at the cathedral organ, a man
missing three fingers rattles souls and benches
      with Franck and Messiaen.
Who told him, "Go ahead, improvise, you will devise
a plan for drawing sunlight from your sacred hands?"

Will I ever learn how to play wild and free with loss,
to fling it into the air like a colorful cap?
Will I ever be able to simply sit and not count the cost?

WHEN WE WERE FOUR

and my twin brother and I got to jumping
on our twin mattresses,
which had lain in boredom on their wooden frames,
we put our agitators in overdrive,
turned our beds into washing machines.
Steam climbed up the wall behind our headboards.
It's hard work shaking the footboard
fast enough to spin-dry a full load.
We seem to have been the first in Berwyn, Pennsylvania
to discover you could do this.
Grampappy Armstrong just clicked his tongue.
Were we the work of the devil?
I told myself I was not afraid of the devil,
but my fear of the devil tasted like horseradish,
and my shame like the smell of sour milk.
Down the street lived a dog named Satan,
who used to shit in our front yard,
and every time my Welsh grandmother said *iechyd da*
right after the grace, it would make me laugh.
Danny Boy could laugh at anything.
We were as quiet as squirrels.
We couldn't sit still at the table
because we had plastic plates and cups
and our chairs had their backs to the wall.
"Father had the shipfitter blues," we bellowed
as the sharp needle of innocence
played through the old 78 of evening
and we trampolined into the limbs of old oaks,
bouncing harder and higher each time,
hoping to stave off night and the ghost of the puppy
who had once fallen through our wild arms.

Venez, vivez avec nous, said the leaves,
promising that stars would bathe us and the sun would dress us.
Gute Nacht, said shirts from a laundry basket,
and the bed slept, holding hands with the water pipes.

from *School for the Blind* (Poets Wear Prada, 2014) and *Border Songs: A Conversation in Poems* (Finishing Line Press, 2017), first appeared in *Wordgathering.*

HOW TO LIVE WELL

(a few guesses)

If you have the choice
to sit squarely in the middle of a cushion
or to straddle the crack between two,
pick the middle of one, but in large matters,
don't set too much store in comfort.
Don't turn on the television
unless you've planned to watch
something particular for days,
and it's still as appetizing
as the smell of Thanksgiving
when you first step into your mother's house.
Sit and do nothing.
Do everything you can.
Don't cry as a way out of taking action.
Don't act as a way out of crying.
Don't confuse bravado with bravery,
or fear with a shortage of courage.
Lay down a line of thought, and then oppose it.
Acquire three heartbreaking mistakes
by the time you turn fifty;
they'll teach you how to be tough
and compassionate at the same time.
Cut yourself at least as many breaks
as you would someone desperately flawed in a novel.
Don't let yourself off the hook
As quickly as you're tempted to.
Read widely and often.
Tear up this list.

COFFEE SHOP

The cashier brought up loss
as he rang up a customer.
"You heard about last night?
It's in this morning's paper."
The customer backed out the door:
"There's nothing you can say," she said.

He kept talking, now to the closed door:
"Except that God works in fucked-up ways.
How else can you explain
a six-year-old crushed by a car
in his driveway, in front of his sister?
"Fucked up, that's all you can say."

I felt a little bad for God. But why
God, when there was so much human suffering nearby?
Was it because I agreed with the man,
but knew I hadn't been equally quick to credit
God for flight and song,
every crow and chrysanthemum?

It would be so much easier to say
the idea of a god is fucked.
Let's just accept, said Nietzsche,
that we are here on our own.
Let's just face, said Feuerbach,
that God's a dead metaphor.

(So, the problem is too much poetry?)

"It killed the firemen," said the man.
"They had to hose the boy off his driveway."
I'd scrub out these silly notions
of God, but then what should I do
with the thrush? Tell me, what should I do
with the firemen who scrubbed the drive?

THE FIDDLER

We sing "How Great Thou Art,"
and Grandma squeezes my hand when they carry you out
in a wheat-covered, farmer's coffin.

I'd wanta cut his dinky off, Mom said
to Grandma when they found out you'd been plowing
the retarded Hoffner girl in the back seat of your car.
The family tribunal around the kitchen table
quoted chapter and verse until it shamed you
upstairs, exiled from your wife, to sleep in a grandson's room.
Better get down on your knees and pray, they said,
and so you did,
rummaging through whispered words until you found
Forgive me, God, forgive me.

What made you do it, Grandpa?
Others asked, but only out of rhetoric.
Had they waited for an answer,
you might have stalled for time,
clanking and cleaning your pipe,
then growled, "Oh, I don't know,"
all grit and gravel,
leaving it at that
so that, a minute later, you could find some chore
to take you to the barn.

Beside your grave, questions mix
with the wind and rain that swirl around us now.
I touch the simple box, smooth, sleek, and narrow
as your fiddle case, and think of what it holds:
hands and knees no longer forced to prayer,
your cock, as quiet as a tractor in the barn,
one more man, misguided, passing through.

A FEW THINGS

I don't know how they keep you on a cross
when they first start the hammering.
I don't know how they make chocolate.
I don't know which parts of a tuna they put in a can
and what they do with the rest.
I don't know what I'll do with the rest of my life.
I don't know any more who sat
behind Bobby Sabol in fourth grade,
but Allen Hawk's dad worked for the phone company.
I don't know why we tell so many sad stories.
I don't know what the Skinheads nextdoor talk about
or what the cockatiel lady likes for lunch.
I've heard that birds resolve disputes through singing contests.
I don't know what a rainbow looks like,
or that my life would be better if I could see one.
I don't know why I'm writing all of this down.
I know all the vegetables in V-8 juice.
There are at least a dozen ways to say "snow" in Inuit.
I know vulnerability is related to hope,
but I can't say how.
I don't know who killed the grooms in Duncan's room.
I don't know at what point you should retire a working dog.
They have three roller coasters at Knoble's Grove.
My mother belly-laughed when we got splashed on The Flume.
Or maybe it's four. I can't remember now.
I don't know why some people give up and others don't.

from *School for the Blind* (Poets Wear Prada, 2014), first appeared in *The Cortland Review*.

WHEN THE CHIPS WERE DOWN

What else they served for lunch that day in the boys' dining room,
I can't say, but, dollars to doughnuts,
whatever they passed off as nutrition was anything but.

It could have been their infamous sausage that greased your shirt
when you first cut into it, or what they called cheese fondue,
made from government surplus Velveeta and powdered eggs.

Whatever it was, we'd have to count on the community bowl
of potato chips at our table for eight to carry us to dinner.

Someone said grace over it because someone had to,
but it was only minutes from then that the clamoring started.
The housemothers stuck to their table in the far corner.
Only Mr. G seemed to size up the situation.

"Satchel Paige didn't have it easy, either, boys," he said.
"Try to save a little for the fella sitting next to you."
He leaned on my shoulder as he said this, and stretched
          for the empty bowl.
"Let me see if the Commandant's in a giving mood."

By this, he meant Miss Brennan, Head of Food Service.
She wasn't, and it didn't take long for their voices to rise
above the general din and crowd it out.

"Brennan, I said these boys need more tater chips."

She said she'd put out all she was going to,
and as Head of Food Service, that was her prerogative.

He repeated, "These boys need more tater chips," and when she shouted
over top of him, he said it again, only this time
like an animal that knew it could break the cage the circus had put it in.

I'd like to tell you that he stormed past her into the kitchen,
that he arranged to bump her accidentally like
          a player might an umpire,

and that he returned, suddenly calm, to set
a full bowl on our table with an "eat up, boys."
It's the stuff of miracles, like turning water into wine,
the stuff that, on the grandest scale, makes for resurrections.

This small thing being, of course, more possible, it might
actually have happened. But, after all that,
after all the intervening years, I don't remember.
After all, it wasn't life or death. After all,
it was just one replaceable man taking a losing
            and inconsequential stand.

By dinner, he was gone, no questions asked, including none by me.
Quit or fired? I can't say. But in church the next Sunday,
when the Scripture was read, I thought I heard him
in the temple, shouting and knocking over tables.

From *School for the Blind* (Poets Wear Prada, 2014).

ACTS OF FAITH

Friends describe colors to me:
trumpets are red they say,
clarinets purple, and oranges
taste like orange. I believe them—
no reason not to.

I buy books to read with equipment for the blind.
It is an act of faith. In the bookstore
all the pages are blank.

At the checkout counter, I pay
with a bill that, earlier,
the grocer said was a twenty.
Or I sign a blank slip
wherever the cashier tells me.

"No big deal," I say to myself
walking out the door.
"Nobody knows everything."
I smell the city—oil and brown.
The yellow sun shines lemonade,
which means the sky must be blue.

From *School for the Blind* (Poets Wear Prada, 2014), first appeared in *Atlanta Review*.

VIGILANCE AND DISSEMBLING

Since I don't see, and have no visual cues,
I'm fascinated by how sighted people dissemble.
I bet they keep their faces unflustered,
while behind their stationary eyes
another set of eyes checks you out.

I say this because, in conversation,
I try to act undivided
while, in fact, I'm on alert
for any glitch in composure—
any revelation of an actor playing a part.

It's often a matter of tone of voice:
most people don't realize it goes even further—
that I'm listening to them breathe,
that I hear body language.
Someone talking with her right hand
while I hold her left
doesn't know how much I know
from the way her body moves,
as if she never touched a tie-line to a dock
and guessed the boat was bobbing up and down.

From *School for the Blind* (Poets Wear Prada, 2014) and *Border Songs: A Conversation in Poems* (Finishing Line Press, 2017), first appeared in *Disability Studies Quarterly*.

WELDON KEES AND THE POSTWAR WORLD

by Robert Zaller

Weldon Kees belongs to the circle of American authors who left us early, in some cases by their own hand: Stephen Crane, Frank Norris, Hart Crane, F. Scott Fitzgerald, Sylvia Plath, Anne Sexton, David Foster Wallace. He was part of a particularly doomed cohort, poets born in the year of World War I, 1914. Randall Jarrell took his life in 1965, wading into traffic. John Berryman committed suicide in 1972. Only William Stafford escaped the curse of that year among poets of significance, living out his natural span.

Weldon Kees disappeared on a July day in 1955, leaving his car parked beside the Golden Gate Bridge, with no note behind. No trace of him was ever found. The assumption, and finally the legal conclusion, was that he had committed suicide. He certainly left the world he'd been living in, where his reputation was still growing. Perhaps that fact alone was all the statement he wished to make. We can't, though, dismiss him with the presumption that, with whatever private demons haunted him, he was after all dismissing us. The poetry compels us to give him attention, and it draws us back not only to the man but the time in and of which he wrote.

Kees came of age in a singularly troubled time. Born into the Great War, he came of age in the Great Depression, the age of totalitarian dictators, and World War II, with its unexampled loss of life and its horrific pendants, the Holocaust and the atomic bomb. The postwar decade was one of revived prosperity, and, for America, dominion over much of the globe. But it was also a time of strife, with great revolutions in Central and East Asia, the collapse of the old imperial order, and, above all, a deep and pervasive anxiety. The atomic age, with its rapidly developing and proliferating thermonuclear arsenals, presented not merely the religious imagination but the practical political world with the prospect of apocalypse. Politicians and generals prepared for nuclear conflict, even as such conflict portended a world without conceivable victors and a planet perhaps unfit for human habitation. Humanity was presented, for the first time, with a situation that could neither be accepted nor avoided. How to live in such a situation, for those most sensitive and alert to it, was a challenge without an apparent solution.

Weldon Kees was multiply gifted, and the restlessness with which he pursued his gifts was not only evidence of a rare energy but of a desperate effort to describe and embrace a world that, in the simplest terms, made no sense. He painted, well enough to be exhibited with the major figures of Abstract Expressionism at their signature gallery, the Peridot. He photographed as well; he made documentaries; he played and composed jazz. He illustrated a book called *Non-Verbal Communication* in collaboration with a California psychiatrist, Jurgen Ruesch, as if to suggest the bankruptcy of words in the moment he faced, and that the bare testimony of images was perhaps all that remained. Yet, at the same time, he was and remained primarily a poet.

Kees published two collections in his lifetime, *The Last Man* and *The Fall of the Magicians*. The first title suggests his own stance in the face of the gathering and then breaking war, the second his bitter response to those, particularly the scientists, whose labors had brought about the end of history: the moment, that is, from which humanity could no longer imagine a future. Kees left behind what might have been a third manuscript, which his editor, Donald Justice, arranged as *Poems 1947-1954*, and some miscellaneous work from various points of his career. The whole makes for a slender volume, 180 pages in all, but not an insubstantial one for a career cut short at forty-one. It was all the poet wished to say, and, although we might desire more it is, in its fragmented way, somehow complete.[1]

The earliest poem printed, dated 1936, suggests many of the themes Kees would develop throughout his work. Its setting is the quintessential community center of the 1930s, a movie palace in which people sat anonymously in the dark and passively consumed a packaged fantasy; its title, "Subtitle," suggests the subordination of word to image that both defined and subverted his poetic project. The tone is alternately ironic and savage; the dead end is already at hand, and, as the poem's speaker notes, there are "No exits":

> We present for you this evening
> A movie of death . . .
>
> Look for no dialogue, or for the
> Sound of any human voice: we have seen fit
> To synchronize this play with

> Squealings of pigs, slow sounds of guns,
> The sharp dead click of chocolatebar machines. . . .
>
> Sit forward, let the screen reveal
> Your heritage, the logic of your destiny.

The talkies were still relatively new at this time, and the seductiveness of spoken dialogue was, in a manner we now lack (or simply take for granted) a fascinating and deeply manipulative part of a film's verisimilitude and the more intimate, 'natural' acting style it enabled. Kees' film replaces this—replaces language—with a suggestion of animals (or humans?) being led to the slaughterhouse, guns rumbling in their lethal sequence, and the fatal click of a mindless technology that offers pleasure but, like the exitless theater itself, locks one into a space without escape, a destiny without hope.

This is still a young man's poem, with a certain rhetorical overbearing and a didacticism that hammers its point home too bluntly, but also with a more careful ear in places and a poet's shrewd capacity for deploying imagery: we may note how the pigs, the guns, and the chocolate machine resonate with each other, cinching the sense of a general trap closing. The "guns" are as yet far away, in a Europe still, as Robinson Jeffers would put it in a premonitory poem of his own "mix[ing] its cups of death,"[2] but, as the chocolate machine's click indicates, already present and 'consumable.'

Speech, for Kees, is not only inadequate, but existentially compromised, corrupted by history, and imposing itself on perception at its very source: for we not only speak but see through words, entangled at the root with what they say. In "Variations on a Theme by Joyce," the opening clause of the poem's repeated line, "The war is in words," suggests the snare of language, which both prefigures action and defines possibility. The "war," that is, is here before it happens in the linguistic imagination through which it takes shape, and in that sense both fully present and never-ending. The overwhelming sense of the 1930s, particularly after Munich, was that the war dreaded since the advent of Hitler was not only inescapable but already underway, lacking only the bloodshed that would soon certify it. Nor, as Kees understood, would America's oceans shield it: distance was nothing to the imagination, and navies not the defenders but the bringers of war.

Pearl Harbor was a year and half off when Kees wrote "June 1940." This was the month of the fall of France, leaving only a beleaguered Britain to face the Nazi onslaught. Despite a still considerable isolationist sentiment on both the left and the right, America was gearing up for war against both major Axis powers. Kees, like Jeffers, saw only horror in the prospect. Enumerating those who had opposed the wars of their times—"Flaubert and Henry James and Owen, / [Randolph] Bourne with his crooked back, Rilke and Lawrence, Joyce"—he, too, excoriated the politicians and quondam pacifists now turned warmongers: "The beaters of drums, the flag-kissing men, whose eyes / Once saw the murder, are washing it clean." Those who could yet see clearly protested now in vain, for, as the poem concludes, "An idiot wind is blowing; the conscience dies."

That isolationism could be an honorable position, indeed as Kees suggested the true defense of "conscience"—has become virtually unrecoverable in the wake of an American triumphalism that, however skeptically some may view our present wars of empire, valorizes World War II as the good and necessary fight for core Western values against the legions of barbarism. But Kees could not set aside the broader context of age-old violence and brutality of which the approaching war seemed only a vaster extension that effaced the very notion of value and brought everything down to itself, "Where the horror of history from cave / To camp to the coffins of yesterday / Burns to a single ash" ("To the North"). Nor was even the bravery of England's fight sufficient against the blood-dimmed tide. In "A Cornucopia for Daily Use," a poem that employs interpolated dialogue, Kees concludes by invoking one of the most celebrated evocations of England as the hope of mankind with a deflating parry that suggests the supersession of value by process:

TWO STRANGERS: We have built Jerusalem in England's green and pleasant land.

AN OLD MAN: I think I see a new process here, a beginning perhaps; the beginning of the end.

The "strangers" declare they have already built Jerusalem in Blake's land, perhaps referring to the Churchillian democracy that Orwell, writing at the same time, thought worth defending with all its flaws; but the old man sees something else at work, the impersonal force he calls "process" that unfolds as fatality, and, without the volition and choice that notionally makes for history, leads only to a final impasse. It is the perception that Yeats had had of "things" in the saddle, riding men, but now applied to a conflict of even greater scale.

The remainder of the poems in *The Last Man* make little overt reference to the war, which came without violent disturbance for most Americans, who pursued their lives with blackouts confined to the coasts and rationing offset by wartime prosperity. They convey nonetheless an insistent note of cultural exhaustion and despair: "The empty and disordered porches hold / The summer's burdened and uneasy death" ("Early Winter"); "the air / Whispering death" ("The Forests'); "Falling night / Will cover all" ("Fugue"). The tone clearly owes something to Eliot, who is directly conjured in "Obituary," but the sense of menace presses hard on that of internal disorder ("assassins dash everywhere," "Stale Weather"; "The paths are guarded by the violent," "Midnight"). The feared invasion takes place not from without but from within, and the final conquest is indistinguishable from surrender. In the climactic poem of the sequence, "The View from the Castle," Kees describes civilization as a ruined redoubt, mortgaged beyond repayment and rotted beyond repair, and ready to rejoin a blood-soaked earth:

> This is the castle then, my dear,
> With its justly famous view.
> There are other historic sights in store—
> Battlegrounds, parks we might explore,
> The hundreds of monuments to war;
> Now that you've seen the castle, my dear,
> We'll see them before we're through.

The poems of *The Fall of the Magicians* continue the themes of *The Last Man,* with its sense of civilization as a charnel house and propaganda replacing speech until animals alone can sense the truth. In "The Contours of Fixation," dogs note that "the odor of blood has a certain appeal" as they crawl home to masters "who are not quite dead," thus connoting a war whose ultimate distillate, bloodsmell, is both its defining measure and its ultimate goal. Leaders, similarly, have assumed the aspect of chimeras whose voices trail off into the howls of their sacrificial victims:

> Applauded monsters, issuing their lies,
> Leap from the mirrors of your home
> Toward the late news, accompanied by screams.
>   ("Moving Target")

The "monsters" not only reflect us, but, 'leaping' from our mirrors, they claim us as themselves, and not even the poet who names them escapes identity: there are no innocent parties, and the victims are only the unlucky. This is not to say that there are no distinctions of guilt, however, and in "Report of the Meeting," Kees focuses on the agents of science, who in an era of destruction bemuse us with promises of elixirs to extend life. Their subject is an aged lion on whom the perfected potion will be tried after endless trials in which "white rats // Learned methods of success or went insane" and the men in their white coats "Experimented with the brains of larks." The ultimate experiment fails; the lion dies. The undaunted scientists, refusing according to their *métier* to concede defeat, continue to study the problem; meanwhile, they "Cut up the lion, placed its parts in pans," and, acknowledging their setback, avoid "the streets for days."

"Report on the Meeting" twists its irony in several ways. The scientists who work to prolong life while death surrounds them on all sides are, in fact, its chief enablers, since the lives they work to save at the expense of creatures great and small are precisely those whose destruction their weapons of war have facilitated. Whether we may read this as well as a commentary on the atomic bomb, or associate Faustian science with the "magicians" whose fall the book's title denotes, no other group comes in for such specific and searing condemnation.

This is not to say, however, that any others are exempted. In "June 1940," Kees had quoted Wilfred Owen to the effect that "All a poet can do today is warn"—that is, discharge the office of a prophet, however vainly. By *The Fall of the Magicians,* art is no longer a sufficient plea, and Kees bids his own fellows goodbye (including, of course, himself):

> Farewell, colleagues of the sublime!
> I greet the welcome papers blowing down a street
> I know too well. Someone has wound the clock,
> Which ticks like a bomb, and is not culpable.
>   ("Dynamite for Operas")

The clock is that of prophecy, and the warning the poet sounds may, like a fire signal, only seem to bring the flames closer by announcing them. Clearly, Kees also has in mind the aestheticism that seeks to avoid 'culpability' by seeking refuge in a purely cognitive realm: Stevens may be his model here. Nonetheless, the product of such activity—of man figured as the "magician" of himself—"ticks like a bomb" as well.

Kees, from this perspective, has no ground to stand on as well. In partial response to this dilemma, he invents a persona in *The Fall of the Magicians* to which he will return in the poems that follow it. He calls him, simply, Robinson, and introduces him by indirection: he is the man who is not there. He has a dog, who stops barking not when Robinson arrives but "after [he] is gone." There's a house, too, well appointed, with a grand piano and "Rugs, vases, panatellas in a humidor." Robinson has traveled; there's a Mexican mirror that, "stuck to the wall / Reflects nothing at all." There's also a bed, and a photograph of a first wife. Nonetheless, we are not to assume that any of this is, unlike the trees rooted in place outside, "actual":

> The pages in the books are blank,
> The books that Robinson has read. That is his favorite chair,
> Or where the chair would be if Robinson were here.

Robinson does rather conjure Stevens here, the sovereign intelligence whose personal bric-a-brac are simply extensions of his own imagination. Even the trees are, as we should be aware in our post-Stevensian world, only "actual," that is, real-seeming rather than ontologically secure. The picture is similarly detailed but no more substantial in "Aspects of Robinson," which finds Kees' subject in New York:

> Robinson walking in the Park, admiring the elephant.
> Robinson buying the *Tribune,* Robinson buying
> the *Times.* Robinson
> Saying "Hello. Yes, this is Robinson."

Robinson is activity, Robinson is assertion, but none of this makes a self. We find him, further, playing cards, taking a taxi, staring downwards from a rooftop, prepared to play golf, describing a tour of Russia, "afraid, drunk, sobbing," and also in bed with a "Mrs. Morse." The inventories go on, culminating in a meticulous account of his dress, his wardrobe, his various appurtenances, and finally "His sad and usual heart." Even the latter, however, is no more than an "aspect" of him, simply another layer in a pile with no bottom. "This is Robinson," as Robinson says, is not an affirmation of identity but the sum of its absence. We infer a well-tailored, well-traveled bourgeois who appears here and there doing this and that, and who answers to a certain set of syllables that connotes a name. But there is no more than that. It is not because there is no individual, substantial reality behind the set of attributes that passes for "Robinson," but that there is no such reality for anyone because there is no longer any civilization to validate it. We are not, Kees suggests, self-authenticating persons in general, but figures composed, linguistically, materially, and morally, of the civilization that grounds and supports us—itself a larger fiction, but one sufficient for purposes of individuation. That civilization had existed, and produced the distinctive intelligences who populate Kees' early verse—Joyce, Proust, Henry James—but it no longer props up the postwar world, having left only simulacra of itself. Robinson can visit the zoo, read his papers, and put on "The jeweled and silent watch that winds itself." He can even contemplate suicide from a roof. But there is not enough of him to genuinely despair, and without despair he cannot even perceive his own derealization, the loss of that which makes persons possible.

"Robinson at Home" comes next, his various figurations appearing as a series of apparitions in sleep that depict the whole human circus:

> Observant scholar, traveller,
> Or uncouth bearded figure squatting in a cave,
> A keen-eyed sniper on the barricades,
> A heretic in catacombs, a famed roué,
> A beggar on the streets, the confidant of Popes—

The waking Robinson identifies with none of these possible selves, but thinks only, "'There is something in this madhouse that I symbolize'"— that is, that he himself, as the sum of the sequence, leads only to further figuration. The poem leads merely to a frighteningly empty prospect in which the empty wind of being blows "long curtains" into a room occupied, finally, only by a void.

The last of the Robinson poems, "Relating to Robinson," finds the poet—
or at any rate the speaker of the poem—appearing to recognize Robinson
on an empty urban street. The speaker knows Robinson is elsewhere, for
it is summer and Robinson spends his summers fashionably; nonetheless, the resemblance is such that he "almost" calls out to him. Coming
abreast, he turns to look at 'Robinson's' face, only to be greeted by "terri-
fying eyes" that stop his blood. The figure speaks disjointedly with horror,
but also with an implied familiarity ("'You must have followed me from
Astor Place'"), the voice suggesting "an echo in the dark." The speaker,
that is to say, recognizes the No One who is both 'Robinson' and himself.
He flees from the apparition, to find himself once more alone.

Robinson may also represent something else, Kees' "last man" who is and
is not the poet himself. He is, at any rate, inseparable from him—not a
proof of existence, but of nightmare. The frightening double who appears
in "Relating to Robinson" becomes a vaguely fragmented series in "Furies,"
whose speaker notes "Not a third who walks beside me / But five or six
more." These latter, this "retinue / of shadows," are a shape-shifting tribe
of monsters, "A harelipped and hunchbacked dwarf / . . . / Who jabbers
the way I do"; a sinister "clown" who turns into "a man with a mouth of
cotton / Trapped in a dentist's chair." Each figure becomes more hideous
than the last, returning the speaker to the terrors of childhood where
"We enter a thousand rooms / That pour the hours back"—a labyrinth
that leads only to the most inexpressibly primal terror of all.

Kees' alienation leads him finally away from the human altogether. From
"Obituary" on, his protagonists more and more often take animal and
insect shapes until they lead to a world populated by them. "The Plague"
represents this process, in which dying locusts suddenly appear, succeeded by unnatural varieties of species, "strange worms crawling; flies
of a kind / We had never seen before / . . . / Queer fungi sprouting." Even
familiar creatures abandon their instinctive ways, until, at the last, a "hideous" swarm of frogs sit "silent and ominous" on each other to listen to
"the sound of rushing wind."

Kees finally settles on the one species both most dubiously domestic and
ferally wild as his ultimate interlocutor, "A monstrous cat that seems / Far
older than the oldest carp / In the waters under the earth," and who intro-

duces himself as "Your spiteful and envenomed shadow" ("Wet Thursday"). We might better think of his true provenance as mythical, a sphinx or a basilisk, the keeper of secrets he does not intend to tell, the face into which one dares not look. The strangeness and unutterability of the world is all that replies to the poet, who seeks the cat out in his lair with an offering in "Colloquy," not expecting any reply but simply reduced to his predicament:

> "I bring,"
> I said, "besides this dish of liver, and an edge
> Of cheese, the customary torments,
> And the usual wonder why we live
> At all, and why the world thins out and perishes
> As it has done for me, sieved
> As I am toward silences. Where
> Are we now? Do we know anything?"

We recognize here the "echo" of Robinson, the modern man without qualities, who asks the question that is only a confession, and gets the response he deserves: "'Give me the dish.'"

If Kees projects his own alienation—both from his kind and from himself—onto menacing animal shapes, he does not forget the reality of man as the dominant species who subjects all others to himself. In "The Clinic," he identifies himself with suffering laboratory animals (cats, again, in this case), being tortured by jolts of electricity:

> Light in the cage like burning foil
> At noon; and I am caught
> With all the other cats that howl
> And dance and spit, lashing their tails
> When the doctors turn the current on.
> The ceiling fries. Waves shimmer from the floor
> Where hell spreads thin between the bars.

The poem proceeds through a catalogue of human ailments, presumably to be investigated by animal experiment, before returning to "that room / Where a room of cats danced, spat, and howled / Upon a burning plate," and concludes, "I was home." 'Home,' that is to say, is where the animal subjects are tortured into mimicking a human activity, dance, even as they writhe and howl with pain; home is "hell," and there is nowhere else.[3]

Blake is again invoked ironically in "Speeches and Lyrics for a Play," not to suggest a new Jerusalem but an atomic ruin: "Geiger counter, clicking soon / In the forests of our noon, / What immortal eye will glimpse / These corpses, and our impotence?" But political references become sparser and sparser in the last poems, and the city, whether of the victor or the vanquished, is a dream of death:

> To build a quiet city in his mind:
> A single overwhelming wish; to build
> Not hastily, for there is so much wind,
> So many eager smilers to be killed.
> ("To Build a Quiet City in His Mind")

The wish for a city, for a worthy humanity, is still there, but the "wind" that permits nothing to stand rises again in the poet's mind, first as an obstacle but then savagely embraced as the wish for a destruction that will at last engulf him too. The vision he has come to is one in which violence permeates everything, and can be turned finally only on oneself: no other exit is possible. The lines in "Place of Execution" take us, precisely, to the place to which Weldon Kees came at last:

> If we walk along the empty foreground of the sea,
> The wind is cold, and there is only darkness at our backs.

If the poet is the canary in the coal mine, then the fate of the cohort of 1914 tells us something about the world that emerged from the Great Depression, World War II, and the postwar world of American empire. Like Kees, Randall Jarrell and John Berryman came to their own ends through a complex combination of circumstances, but a common thread of isolation and alienation runs through their work, and the title of one of Jarrell's last works, *A Sad Heart at the Supermarket*, epitomizes the sense of what Kees himself called in "The Clinic" the "desiccation" of modern life. At the juncture where we ourselves stand, with an empire that has metastatized around the globe, an ethos of empty consumption, and a social infrastructure that is crumbling visibly beneath us, Kees' work is both a warning and a challenge.

Notes

1. All subsequent references are to Donald Justice, ed., *The Collected Poems of Weldon Kees* (Lincoln and London: University of Nebraska Press, 1975).

2. "Hellenistics," in Tim Hunt, ed., *The Collected Poetry of Robinson Jeffers*, 5 vols. (Stanford, CA: Stanford University Press, 1988-2001), 2: 526-28. Cited as *CPRJ*.

3. *Cf.* Jeffers' similar and earlier-written poem, "Memoir" (*CPRJ* 2: 524-25), with which Kees may well have been familiar, and also "The King of Beasts" (3: 138).

ALMOST MORNING

Juditha Dowd

Again I wake to your heat
       your scent of wood smoke

your body   as familiar as my own
       and yet a mystery

touch me   yes
              and here

I am your cello
       bowed allegro moderato

I am your wild persimmon sweet and ripe

from Dowd's manuscript "Audubon's Sparrow"—
written in the voice of Lucy Bakewell, Audubon's wife.

LIGHT

Juditha Dowd

          There

on the limb of that red-leafed tree

you have taught me to see
        not only the cardinal

but light itself
        and the wind in it

Now as I move through Father's fields
the wheat divides
        weighs against my thighs
            like water in a creek

        like a hand might
            if it brushed me

unintentionally

From Dowd's manuscript "Audubon's Sparrow"—
written in the voice of Lucy Bakewell, Audubon's wife

WHEATFIELD WITH CROWS

(Vincent van Gogh, oil painting, 1890)

Alfred Encarnacion

If this is the last painting of your life, how could it not unleash
A turbulent sky to match the maelstrom building inside of you?
If your thoughts are scattered and wind-driven by the grind—
The ten thousand things—how could crows not be the perfect
Embodiment of your angst? The eye travels that road going
Nowhere through blazing wheat, like yellow wavering flames,
Pulled toward whatever waits at the heart of the field, if anything
Awaits other than the Abyss. *Gaze into it long enough*
& it stares back into you. Sad Vincent, what did you see
That would soon end your life? What did you hear in the livid
Sky of no resurrection but the cawing, cawing, calling
Of crows, crows, so many crows?

FINDING A BLUEBIRD EGG

Joseph Cilluffo

The egg was cracked.
In fact, it was halved, or nearly so.
The outside of each half was smooth
and that certain blue
you only find on eggs
and nowhere else,
not even eyes, not even
a newborn's eyes (which themselves
are a blue seen nowhere else).
The inside of the shell
was white and clean with no trace
of yolk. It seemed too early in the season
for a bluebird hatchling, and my mind,
stuck in winter, goes dark
—was the egg cracked
by the bird going out, or
something getting in?
Stop. Begin the thought again.
It's springtime. Easter has just passed.
But it's cold comfort, to know
how even dying is breaking free.

IGNITION

Grant Clauser

Like a museum, the pre-owned lot displays
stories of starts and stops.
Old cars with tires polished black
crack in the sun, their odometers
spun back a few turns on the dial.
We ask about the American truck,
the Japanese sedan, kick the tires
as if that air-filled thud could tell us,
like a palm reading, what kind of luck
these wheels may bring.
I wonder what my father would say,
weighing mileage over years, how long
it takes a thing to reach its peak and then
decline, how they try to hide rust
with cheap paint or mask years
of cigarettes with a dose of something
stronger. My daughter, still hope and wonder,
glides from car to car and pictures herself
on the road, right foot forward
bearing down on the highway
to a place another state away.
When she shifts into drive
the engine answers: *where?*
I try but can't tell her
there's nothing new here,
just new to her.
No matter how old,
the keys to the car
are always shiny.

TO THE ELDERLY PARISHIONER I FOUND HEMORRHAGING IN THE CHURCH YARD

Joseph A. Chelius

How resourceful of me in that time before cell phones
to run to church
where Monsignor in a black cassock
was molding into altar boys
a slouching row of indifferent 8th graders—
boys who preferred nothing better on Saturday mornings
than to scrap on the courts with hockey sticks.

And how impressed you might have been
by my self-restraint,
holding by the strings
a box of assorted bakery cookies
while Monsignor, with a heavy patience,
edified at the tabernacle—
raising the gold chalice and intoning in the voice
he used for sermons.

God provides, it can be said with certainty,
so it would have pleased you to know
that He'd chosen as messenger
a boy trained by the Sisters of the Immaculate Heart

to murmur a prayer when an ambulance passed,
nod deferentially at every mention of Jesus,
who stood among the stained glass depictions
of the Stations of the Cross
like a respectful servant or customer in line,

unwilling to call out
(at least not without putting up his hand)
to a priest during the holy tutorial of boys
whose brutal slap shots lifted off asphalt,
whose shrill oaths resounded off buildings—
boys bold, brazen, quick to speak out of turn—
the wrong sorts of messenger
whom God might have sent.

BEFORE THE EAGLES GAME

Joseph A. Chelius

It was safe to say
as I shopped at Acme
for cold cuts and chips
that the artisan loaves
on a rack by the deli
gave me no urge
before the stunned crowd
of Sunday shoppers
to connect on a slant route
with a man in a jeff cap
as he pushed his cart
toward the end zone
of the checkout.

And that I felt no flutter
on passing #20
(a bit paunchy in his jersey)
as he stood fixated
at the meat case—
wholly in the moment
of surveying steaks,

Behind the store a row of bales
against the stucco wall
bore no resemblance
to the immutable force
of an offensive line,
nor did some bees I glimpsed
whooping it up
over produce boxes
piled in the driveway
put me in mind

of the Steelers' cheerleaders—
in their detestable colors
of black and gold.

No football zealot,
no bleeder of green,
I could say with conviction
that a formation of geese
I saw flying above me
just minutes before kickoff at 4:25
did not quicken my pulse,
nor seem anything at all
like the Eagles players
led by their quarterback
as they streamed across
the field of the sky.

MY FATHER'S BELONGINGS

Joseph Cilluffo

Of all the things I threw away
cleaning out my father's apartment,
the one I could not bear to lose
was his brush. The oval
of polished sandalwood,
just the right size for a strong palm.
Its short boar-hair, plush and still holding
one or two of his own. It is
a magnificent brush. This is not
the tool of a man who could no longer
groom himself. The wood is smooth
and worn just a little
where it had been gripped countless times
—a ritual, reverent, imprinted
on the grain. I can turn it over,
run a thumb across
stiff bristles to feel
just a little pain.

SPENT

Joseph Cilluffo

I spent the day
in the graveyard,
in the shadow
of your stone.
Or at least
I spent a few hours,
long enough that the shadow
grew long around me.
Or at least
the shadow grew oppressive
with the sound
of you not speaking.
It wasn't long.
I spent an hour
in the graveyard,
stretched across your stone.
Or perhaps minutes.
A moment.
The sun didn't move
and you didn't move,
and there was no sound
but the sound of me leaving,
and of you, already gone.

LUNCH AT THE A&N DINER

for Linda Titus
November 5th, 2016

W.D. Ehrhart

Miss Bowers? Holy cow! Fourth grade
was sixty years ago. Surprised we still
remember back that far. Mrs. Vera.
Mrs. Kulp. Then junior high
and high school: Pennridge Rams.
So much we shared while we were
growing up, good times and bad.
But every generation comes of age.
And then grows old, looks back,
and wonders how it all went by
so quickly. And so long ago.
Suzie died before she started college.
Kenny died in Vietnam. That brilliant
girl who played the flute became
an alcoholic. Gareth died of AIDS.
But that's the way it goes.
I'd rather think about one
summer night we spent together
after I came back from war and you
from school, old friends already,
even then, though youngsters still,
come morning went our separate ways.
Yet here we are again. Just you and me.
What lunchtime crowd? They don't exist.
That night was refuge from the storm
that raged inside of me for years.
The war was undescribable.
Being home was worse.
You were playing a harp.
You had wings that night.
And a halo.
You still do.

THE PIC ON A PC SCREEN

Alfred Encarnacion

> *A young man… with the joy of being immortal in his eyes*
> —C.P. Cavafy, "One of Their Gods"

I found it not quite by chance

obsessing over those Google images,

hoping that somehow E's face might appear.

Then without warning it was there.

Forty years had passed but

I knew it instantly and froze

unable to draw a breath.

That face changed almost beyond

recognition, yet something familiar—

despite the desertion of youth—lurked

in the tilt of the head, the inquisitive smile.

The eyes' dark circles, bloated

cheeks, steel gray hair—relentless

reminders that even the beautiful

must relinquish their claim to beauty

and become merely mortal like those

gods of antiquity who transformed them-

selves to walk among us unnoticed.

RELICS

for john donne

Tree Riesener

they will take it away
the gravely delicate floral linen dress
your child thought suitable
for your grave
after all these years still bright
where they unpicked the stitches
turned back the seam to show its lasting beauty
everything that was given to the quiet grave
will be illuminated on their stage
exposed and naked your pretty ivory bones
that came unstrung
they'll re-connect with silver wire
and hang up on their gallows
they'll take away
your only salvaged dignity
the bright bracelet of coral beads
alternating with saved white birth letters
that spell your name
in their glass exhibit case
it will say *I was*
a fact they cannot take away

THE TIGHTROPE WALKER

David Adès

The tightrope walker regulates his breath,

hums his mantras, knows his chakras,
seeks balance in all things.

He has practiced and practiced calmness,

learnt to slow his heart beat,
to empty his mind of errant thought

knowing that each step on the wire

might be his last, that one stumble,
one graceless fall will end it all.

There is no life without risk.

He risks in order to live, and living,
lives in order to risk, always

on some edge, some deep precipice,

embracing the idea of flight, loving
like this too, fearful, exhilarated.

AMERICANA

Bob Evans

Sometimes I see eagles.
A bald taking flight from
the middle of the road.
A golden perched
on the carcass of a deer.
Mostly, I see vultures
wheeling overhead on thermals.
Heads featherless to cleanly
burrow into viscera.
Their only natural means of defense,
projectile vomiting. When it's hot,
they piss on themselves to keep cool
and spread their wings as if they belonged
on the back of some dark doubloon.
They'll flock in a single tree
and return there like fruit each year.
Down the road they perch
on the First Presbyterian steeple
like metaphors. Every time
I see one fly, I think *eagle*
and am disappointed.
Every time they see me pass
they're disappointed but think
We'll wait.

FIRE IN THE SKY

Joyce Meyers

Gunshots? Bombs?
Merely thunder?
Dark blanket of dread,
then explosion of red
cascades against black sky,
to sighs of relief,
gasps of delight.

The burst of elation
erases all reason,
blurs the cause
for celebration:
bombs bursting in air,
bodies bloodied,
sprawled beneath a flag,
still there.

Gems against black velvet
falling into trees
fill the sky with smoke,
blot out the truth of stars.

When morning comes
the sky is blue and clear
as on the day the planes
flew into buildings,
toppled every certainty.

Biggest stars, like empires,
shine most brightly
just before they die,
brighten the sky with
fireworks, supernovas.
Just ask a black hole
what it knows of apocalypse,
the gravitational pull
of darkness.

ALONG THE OHIO

Richard Luftig

This river with so many meanders,
and oxbows that at times it seems
like it has no idea which way
to flow. And the towns

that run along; confused,
without direction as if
folks believe that if
the damn water would just

straighten itself out, run
pure and plumb, folks
might see what they need
to save the place, keep

things ahead of the curve.
But here, at Coropolis, Crown City,
Maysville and Martin's Ferry,
the deserted, boarded-up stores

show their rears to the river
and the banks seem to have lost
any interest in watching water pass
downstream. The only occupants

left are bald tires,
rusting oil drums,
broken quart bottles of High Life
and the occasional sofa

dumped when people thought
no one was looking. Even the houses
seem to have given up
the ghost: back yards

scattered with driftwood
and weeds, save for one
with an ornament of a fat,
old, Dutch woman bending

over her tulips, bloomers
mooning the water and a family
of plastic ducks wondering
when it will be their turn to leave.

ON READING KEROUAC'S *BIG SUR* AGAIN AFTER SIXTEEN YEARS

Jacob Riyeff

St. John's day 2016 and the grey
salt-crusted streets of Milwaukee
welcome us home—a wife and two kids
in back, a third growing in the dark wet
of her womb. The biting cold funnels
between old multi-level houses split into
flats that Poles built nearly a century
ago. And opening a reissue of *Big Sur*
from Penguin raises phantoms
from youth, bearded ecstatic youth,
that hang thick just below the surface—
Chris, who suffers good-naturedly in his
flannel shirts, and Steve who went into
the Air Force, and Paul who loved sound
poetry, and someone I won't name who
tried harder than most. And we had
the chance to be "real" bohemians then—
To rush headlong into the sullen drunken
madness Jack describes, as he hides
from all the sad mess of the world
that no one can speak to anymore—
And it's gone and getting bigger for sixty years.
There were visions and spontaneous campouts
in Boulder foothills—drumming and golden dreams
spread over our shoulders like hidden
green scapulars. A naïve thirst
for everything and a giddy call in the bones
suffocating for joy in the gone night,
driving for days to see acquaintances spread thru-out
the country, working on vegetable farms, sleeping
in Iowa campgrounds with the Great Blue Heron ruling over

the lazing river every beatific twilight—
But unlike Jack and his grim buddies,
most of us veered off course, kept ourselves
from the dark roses of the unborn—
And on this side of that Great Divide all-holy
we're hugging our Golden Eternity quietly in brief
moments between toddlers' incessant questions,
giant timeblocks of small hands and running,
and doing the next square thing. And maybe
Jack's with St. Michael right now, thinking,
"O, thank God!"—

THE COMFORT OF DESIGN

Judy Kronenfeld

The great swell stretches wide
its maw in Hokusai's *Under the Wave*
off Kanagawa; its finger-like froth
hooks to whelm the boats
that ride in its trough,
and the shallow shells in which the oarsmen
double over themselves echo,
but are dwarfed by the huge roar
of that monstrous concave.

Yet, the palate of the wave is striped
quite evenly in light and navy
blue, and the ragged fluffs of white foam
could be polka-dots
on a bolt of rippling dark-dyed silk,
and the foreground white-caped
surge—that mirrors Mt. Fuji
in the distance—resembles a hill
of vanilla ice cream beginning to melt
in a deep bowl.

Imminent disaster flattens
with stressed edges and uniform
light—the artist's sign in the upper
left corner part of an almost frozen
scheme. The terror of the monster wave
nearly subsides in the woodcut's designs,
"between the lines," as in childhood's
coloring books and tales—

where the dragon breathes out fire
in tendrils, and the trees and moss swallowing
the sleeper's castle are green symmetrical
dashes and dots, and the skin of the frog

the princess finds revolting
is as intricately patterned as her gown—

as if the world can tame
terror, death, catastrophe, hate,
and is made mainly for delight:
served up gratis

as a surprise cake, thrillingly
embellished with roses, shells,
stars, waves.

A-N-D-R-E-A

Sandra Becker

It could be Atlanta, Chicago, or LA.
    It's Front Street in Plainfield, New Jersey.
There are likely nice cars and houses around the corner,
    a sign that reads *Safe neighborhoods save lives.*
She could be Russian, Mexican, Thai;
    she doesn't know where she's from,
her name, or her age.
    She could be Sylvia, Minerva, Carmen.
She calls herself Andrea.
    She may have been abandoned,
abducted, sold for cash.
    Only four then, she may have been
traded, hunted, kidnapped, ensnared.
    Too young to have fallen
for the promise of acting, modeling,
    waitressing in Paris, the dream
of school, an apartment, a Mercedes,
    lured El Norte by a pimp of Los Leños,
forced into a car in Via Lactea, the Milky Way.
    In every house, there is a devil,
says the Mexican official to this reporter,
    about the police who enable it.

There might be a middle-class family
    behind this locked basement door.
There are likely children playing
    around the block on a swing or a sliding pond.

This could have been a childhood.
　　You get *broken* by your captors, *locked-down*
in a gated villa in Ensenada or Tijuana.
　　You cross the border, say a prayer to St. Jude,
the patron saint of lost causes. You're forced
　　to trudge twelve miles across the hills
where J-E-S-U-S is spelled out in rocks
　　ten feet high on your way to the Gates of Hell.
It could be Howard Johnson's, the Crowne Plaza,
　　the Radisson Casa Grande.
It could be a stash house in Queens or Union City,
　　San Diego, or Vista, California.
There might be a man who reads Bible passages
　　before and after he takes you.
The ceiling may be painted an azure blue,
　　tiled in circles of suns and moons.
The ceiling may be marked with pocks
　　of chipping paint or adorned with flowers in appliqué.
You might look free in Disneyland
　　where you're taken routinely to each strange man,
and follow orders to take his hand and say,
　　I've been looking for you, daddy,
but you are bound by invisible shackles.
　　The cuts you make in your arms
with the knife might spell anything—
　　why not A-N-D-R-E-A?

CAPTIVITY

Diana Pazicky

When I approach, two Oscar fish surge,
fins fanning wildly like sails in the wind.
They stare at me, perhaps hoping I'll feed them,
perhaps to break up the Sisyphean monotony
of a journey back and forth between glass walls,
tantalizing barricades to vistas they cannot reach.
Like hamsters spinning on the wheel,
they conjure up the definition of insanity.

"He" (I assume from his large size)
is a blend of lacquered black and brown
streaked with magisterial gold lame.
His bulging eyes are dark except when light
catches them, uses its alchemy to turn them
into golden beams flashing on and off
as he executes slow, graceful pirouettes
propelled by pale gray fins, translucent veils.

"She" is a delicate, miniature version of him,
ebony but decorated with iridescent speckles
of emerald, gold, and turquoise, looking like
a peacock that dove by mistake into the water.
Lithe and limber, she moves faster than he,
flutters the gossamer filigree of fins and tail
with nervous energy, as she circles the tank
and the lump of fake black driftwood.

I wonder, do they pass by
in oblivion, or do they depend
on each other, at the very least
for the dim solace of presence?
Would one miss the other if it died?
Or is this just another bad marriage
in which lonely couples circle,
swim their separate channels?

CLARITY

Marie Kane

Do not lose sight of distant lights
        on a sea—fragments of spirit—
        rising and falling, cresting
and dropping—they may yet save you.

Wild sea pulls sand out in storms—
        do not lose the sand within
        that sounds your depth—
it may yet build the unexpected:

Rilke says, *all is known to you*—
        the wildness of the open ocean,
        or the becalmed, polished surface.
Trace those heights, complete
        that journey—create your sand
        castles (soon to be ocean-absorbed),

but first, enclose purple or blue sea glass
        in their walls so that when we
        knock, the door opens—
and we cross the splendid threshold—
        undulating, gills forming, learning
        the roads of the sea.

APOLOGIA

Linda M. Fischer

You ask if I'm still not up to writing
with: *should I start to worry yet?*
like a solicitous mother who would press
her lips to a child's forehead thinking
she might be ill. Not today. No,
not on a day when the air ripples
like silk, fragrant with overnight rain—
gardens kindled by a splash of sunlight,
the civilities of greenness at my feet.

How to explain an interlude of seamless
peace in a world of turmoil…only that I,
fugitive from imperatives, choose
to steep myself in a sea of serenity,
bed in the clover of an ordered life—
the solidity of bricks and mortar,
the harmony of succulents I group
with cactus to set out in clay pots.
More than this? To simply live.

POETRY 101

Joyce Meyers

forget destinations
mapless, the body
a compass
track magnetic forces
fear the dark
enter caves
become a glowworm
a bat
sprout wings

go barefoot
in the garden
kneel in the dirt
dig deep
get fingers caked
with loam
taste every seed
plant some bitter ones
pray for rain

use a jagged edge
to cut the heart
of dreams
get bloody
free words tethered
by strands
of gossamer
and gut

start with a recipe
discard it
play with ingredients
find what nourishes
chop onions, never stop
to wipe tears

season with pepper
vinegar honey
spice, essence
of everything
simmer as long
as it takes
for truth
to bubble up

THE POETRY OF SCIENCE

W.D. Ehrhart

> *"Science is the poetry of reality."*
> —Richard Dawkins

Was it Ptolemy who posited
the music of the spheres?
Aristotle guessed there must be atoms.
Galen gave us medicine
while Archimedes gave the world "Eureka!"
Galileo used a glass to prove
Copernicus and Kepler had it right.
Leonardo knew that men would fly.
Descartes, the French philosopher,
could think because he was,
and what is science, after all,
but natural philosophy?
An apple fell on Newton's head,
symbolism Isaac took to heart.
Smith's map of Britain changed the world.
Darwin grasped that men and monkeys
aren't so different as we'd like to think
while Lister gave us more than Listerine.
Indeed, the world would be bereft
of poetry if mass times speed times
speed again were not the perfect poem.
And if you're not convinced, consider this:
Madame Curie's burning passion killed her.
How much more poetic can you get?

IN THE SNOW

Linda M. Fischer

Under cover of night, winter's alchemy
transforms the terrain—drifts of powder
punctuated by tufts of fountain grass,
ferns sticking up like rusty nails.
Unemptied trash bins huddle at the curb
under white turbans, solemn as Wazirs.
Not a sign of life anywhere except for squirrels
skittering over the frosted limbs of a maple,
scattering snow in their wake—neighbors
not yet afoot, reluctant to venture outside
until a bright sun softens the landscape.

Only the young seem to delight in snow,
eager to embrace Nature's windfall—days
as a child I waited for my friends to appear
so we could drag our sleds to a nearby golf
course and ply their runners on the Big Hill,
hardening it to an icy slick, until nightfall
drove us home—our leggings soaked,
faces wind-chapped, fingers numb—mine
nearly frostbitten once until a kind boy
I knew saw me close to tears and chafed
them long enough to make the blood flow.

The advent of snow still holds me in awe,
tinged with the shiver of anticipation I felt
at the prospect of being sprung from routine—
the tedium of school—my quotidian expectations
overturned, now as then, by the mysterious
workings of the universe: the snow's deeps
akin to the northern latitudes of my youth.
This morning, a virgin landscape compels me;
I sally forth in a pair of old boots and a snug
down jacket. Drawing in the clean crisp smell
of snow-cleansed air, I reach for the shovel.

SANTA, DELAYED

Joseph A. Chelius

By mid-February all the ornaments
on Wyandotte Street have been put away
except for a giant Santa at the corner house.
Driving by I glimpse him at the chimney top
in his wrinkled valor,
empty sack slung over one shoulder
as if waiting for the sleigh to pick him up.

It was weeks ago that the rest of us,
bloated on craft beer and fruit cake,
returned to the construction site
and to the blank faces of our monitors,
but here he is as if emerging in the gray weather,
assaulted by sleet and bird droppings,
causing us to wonder if his team
has played a prank and left him behind,
or if he has been sidetracked all this time
by a family with zesty snacks
and a robust entertainment center.

Easy to picture him with his lips moving,
rehearsing excuses for Mrs. Claus,
but what to tell the young elves—
enterprising designers and assemblers, impressionable interns—
for whom he should be setting an example?

Already he has missed the post-holiday blues party
and the chance to extend
along with the bonus checks
a few Atta boys to the unsung heroes in Packaging.

Missed, too, the post-mortem in the conference room
dubbed The Workshop
where the department heads gather annually
for a long PowerPoint on the past season's highlights,
emphasizing the positive,
though touching on what they might have done better.

And moving forward, as they like to say,
how they might exceed this year's target goals
regarding production, deliverables—
the Wow factor.

APOLOGY TO TIME

Bob Evans

We who have cursed you
for leaving us too soon and for
congealing like marrow around us,
we who see that you get wasted,
a pledge allowed neither sleep nor sobriety,
we who tried to conquer you
with sand and shadows,
gears and cogs,
microchips and diodes,
we who mark you, waste you,
limit you and beat you,
use your signatures as our own,
we who end up doing you because
we've already done something worse,
we who rest when you are out
and expire when you are up
apologize for killing you when young
and for trying to turn back your hands
when all you wanted to do was fly.

BEYOND IMITATION

by Erik Greinke

Everyone knows that poetry underwent a radical deconstruction with the advent of modernism. The poetic conventions of rhyme and meter were the primary losses. Efforts by new formalists notwithstanding, the rhyme and meter of the pre-moderns has been replaced by the conventions of free verse, but many of theses conventions have become so rigid that they are now in themselves a type of free verse formalism.

Conventions are always temporary. Progress requires new, ever evolving approaches, whether in art, science or politics. Everything has both an up and a down side. In my 70th year, I still haven't found an exception to the yin-yang principle.

1. Classic or Cliché?

Some conventions devolve into cliché rather quickly. I'm thinking of the idiosyncrasies of e. e. cummings. His experimental breakage of grammatical rules reinforced the content and energy of *his* poems. His use of the lower case for personal nouns had meaning in the overall context of *his* work. It was innovative and made a statement within cummings' personal style. Many of his poems may rightfully be called "classics."

Cummings knew what he was doing, but those who attempted to adopt his stylistic choices as conventions to be used in their own work are unoriginal and it is likely that their work is derivative in more ways than one, resulting in a cliché instead of a classic. One size has never fit all. It's unfortunate for the general state of the art that many young poets seem to think that writing in lower case is, or should be, standard practice. A cliché is a tired classic. What works in one period of time may fall flat in a later one. This is both inevitable and desirable, because as poets, we need to support and contribute to the potential of poetry.

The larger and most basic issue is received information and its interference with the creative process, a process that requires originality. Imitation can be a double-edged sword. So can originality. Most beginning poets go through a period of imitation. During this process, poets are susceptible to *received information infection*. The infection can be persistent over a long lifetime of writing. It can be without obvious symptoms to the infected whose work becomes affected and clichéd. Ironically, this may make it more publishable.

Received information affects writer and reader alike. Though we give lip service to originality, we may not like it when we get it. Experimental poetry is the least popular category of the art. Only a handful of poets describe themselves as "experimental," far less than one percent. MFA programs unintentionally exacerbate the strong bias against originality, because they reinforce current conventions in an art that has, as its very nature, a need for innovation and originality. The bastardization of the style of e. e. cummings comes again to mind in this regard as an example of an original and experimental poet whose style became highly imitated by younger poets who, in turn, created works deeply infected by cliché.

It all leads back, full circle, to clichés. We need an expanded definition. "Deep clichés" go largely unnoticed. A definition limited to stylistic elements ignores the essence of what a cliché is. A cliché in this sense can be predictable format, pattern or metaphor. An immediate example is the pattern followed by elder poets who (predictably) focus on the past or on impending death or a young poet's equally predictable love poems.

The content of a poem may be seen as a cliché if it follows a predictable pattern or metaphor. Many more works than those commonly perceived as clichés would be included in that category if this expanded definition became widespread. A cliché is a chameleon that changes coloration to fit into its environment.

The solution is not for poets to avoid the "great themes" of love and death, but for them to write better about those themes, thus creating new classics that are relevant to the current zeitgeist.

But originality has its problems, too. "Accessibility" can be a code word for "simple and prosaic," but works that depart radically from current conventions may be too difficult or subjective. The very act of submitting for publication means that the poet is attempting to communicate *something*. If an experimental poem is highly off-putting, that may, ironically, be its value and its statement. Although this is a legitimate value in poetry, it has never been a popular one, implying that people don't generally read poetry to be alienated or confused. Perhaps "all things in moderation," itself a cliché, may be the best wisdom. Some poets like to show more skin than others. Some are nudists and some wear thick armor or elaborate costumes, according to personal taste.

2. Specificity

In my experience, Nature does indeed abhor a vacuum. I know my Pekingese (aka "dog") does, as a representative of the animals. She tries to bite it. The vacuum created by the modernist deconstruction of the poetic conventions of rhyme and meter left poets little choice for stylistic variation. A new emphasis on imagery, advocated and practiced by H. D., Amy Lowell, Ezra Pound, Wallace Stevens, T. S. Eliot and other imagists became a new free-verse formalism with its own rigid standards.

The convention developed that images be specific and particular. Rather than use the ambiguous "stone" in a poem, a specific *kind* of stone should be used, granite, sandstone or shale. I live in Michigan, where there are eighty varieties of large trees. I do not know all their names. Specificity often works against the universal appeal of the poem, which should be, in my opinion, the priority.

"Stone" signifies a higher level of abstraction than the more specific "granite." Used in a poem, the more ambiguous "stone" reinforces a higher level of abstract awareness and imagistic receptivity in the imagination of the reader-poet. Every word used in a poem is a seed planted in the imaginative soil provided by its reader. Increased reader participation is highly desirable in poetry. Good poetry stimulates new emotional and intellectual perspectives which in turn expand the reader's personal and social awareness.

A group of us sat around, talking about music. A pretentious interloper kept referring to his guitar as his "Fender." After he left, a non-musician friend asked me why the guy kept trying to bring car parts into the conversation. When I explained, he said, "Why didn't he just say 'guitar'?" This illustrates how specificity leads to snobbism.

At the very least, specificity narrows the participation of the reader, like traditional prose. Ironically, poetry that is more prosaic is seen as more accessible, as in the example of the narrative poem, yet that kind of accessibility can remove the mystery and ambiguity which are essential to poetry and which form the primary distinction between poetry and prose.

When is specificity good, then? The answer is that it is only a good principle to follow when it contributes to the primary theme and/or metaphor of a poem. Used surgically, it can be invaluable. Overused, it dulls the main thrust of the poem. Poems that completely lack specificity are reliant on what remains, good or bad. Stripped of specific images, a non-narrative, imagistic poem becomes a lyrical statement. A lyric poem tends to make a more abstract statement than a narrative poem does. Music becomes a priority then. Poets should strive to be aware of these dynamics, especially during revision, when the excitement of initial inspiration has calmed.

One meaningful measure of universality in a poem is how easily it translates into foreign languages. The major skill required of a translator of poetry is the ability to choose the word that matches the emotional and intellectual nuances of the word in the original language from a list of its synonyms in the intended foreign language. Although synonyms are words that mean roughly the same thing, each synonym has a different nuance. Nuance is a central value of poetry. Subtle differences matter, sometimes a great deal.

Will international readers relate more to "stone" or "granite?" I like my readers to participate in the poem. "Stone," being a generality (as opposed to the more specific "granite"), not only translates more easily to a foreign language, but it also allows the reader to *imagine* the specific type of stone that he or she relates best to, thus lubricating the movement of the poem toward the final line/revelation/resolution. I believe that a poem does not happen on a page, but rather in the mind of its reader. If a reader has to supply his own kind of "stone," he participates in the poem on an *imaginary level*. This is the creative state of mind a poem needs in order to be received. Initially, it is the poet who receives the inspirational impulse. He then transmits that state, if he can, to his readers. Ideally, the poem happens (again) in the mind of the reader, and the reader may become a degree more open-minded.

Prosaic accessibility is not the same as poetic accessibility. Specificity increases the accessibility of prose but it also decreases accessibility to those imaginative and creative states of mind where poems happen. The best rule of thumb for me is to include only images which support and reinforce the main emotional thrust of the poem. Ambiguous images stimulate a reader's imagination better than images that are too categorical and so specific that they rely on a similarity of knowledge and experiential base in their readers.

3. Persona

A poet of my acquaintance who is also an AIDS counselor, is writing a series of poems from the points of view of her clients. The worthiness of her project is clear. It helps her to "walk a mile in their moccasins," to improve her understanding of her clients and relate to them better. Readers of the poems will have similar benefits, and the series is a blow against fear and prejudice too. But there is a side effect. People persist in interpreting the poems as autobiographically "true." They think she has AIDS. My friend always explains that the poems are "persona poems," true in a higher, more abstract sense, but not autobiographical.

While it is understandable that general readers might not understand what has long been called "poetic license," it is lamentable when the confusion extends to poets who consider themselves serious. This is an example of a convention that is becoming rigid and that restricts poetic freedom and imagination.

Confessional poets such as William Snodgrass, Robert Lowell, Sylvia Plath, Anne Sexton and Allen Ginsberg adhered to a non-fictional, autobiographical standard that affected later poets who wrote in the first-person, autobiographical narrative. Narcissistic navel-gazing has infected the art like a virus, especially in the Post-Beat underground literary scene. Once again, received information has interfered with originality and imaginative creativity, to the detriment of the art.

Stylistic affectations and other received information that is too often used out of context draw attention to themselves without justification, and too often distract from the primary metaphor of a poem. Also, these affectations, despite being intended as a display of the poet's sophistication, have the opposite effect, instead verifying the poet's naivete and unoriginality.

"Art" equals "artifice" equals "artificial." Imagination and fantasy are essential to art. Why do we have a growing consensus (becoming a convention) that insists on an essentially non-fictional approach to narrative poetry? The answer is *imitation*. Consensus and convention are a slippery slope, in this case sliding away from the very elements that distinguish poetry from prose.

Within prose, between fiction and non-fiction, fiction has traditionally been seen as the more artistic. The current trend has been toward "creative non-fiction" over the past few decades. The charge was led by Truman Capote, Tom Wolfe and Hunter S. Thompson, journalists who brought fictional elements into non-fiction, using personal opinion, anecdote, hyperbole and direct participation to give their "reports" more personality, immediacy and entertainment value. Oddly, poetry, long considered the artiest type of writing, has proceeded significantly in the other direction. Is veracity a better value for an art based in imagination, or is it an erosion of the essence of poetry itself, maybe even the beginning of the end?

I don't know the answer to this, but it's a damn good question. I do know that if a poet adheres to current dogma, his poems cannot transcend much beyond the obvious. Maybe the first step toward a more universal poetry is to move beyond imitation.

The problem of originality versus received information is the larger issue at hand. Imitation is a necessary stage of poetic development, but a poet who remains stuck at that stage can never achieve his full potential, and this deprives the art itself of what he might have contributed.

IN MEMORY OF
YEVGENY ALEKSANDROVICH YEVTUSHENKO
(1932-2017)*

by Valentina Sinkevich

Yevgeny Yevtushenko died on April 1 in Tulsa, Oklahoma.

Let me say immediately that I consider this extraordinarily and variously gifted person a striking phenomenon, a poet who is much more than a poet—not only in Russia. It's a shame Mother Nature publishes people like him in such microscopic print runs. I had the good fortune to meet Yevgeny Yevtushenko in person. And in the last period of his life, a complicated time for him, we would carry on long telephone conversations fairly often, sometimes for more than two hours. I'll try to rely once again on my ninety-year-old memory and share with readers some impressions of my brief meetings with him in the past, and to resurrect something from our quite recent telephone conversations.

I saw Yevtushenko for the first time fifty-one years ago, during his first visit to America in 1966. He was reading at Queens College in New York and also at some Jewish cultural center closer to the train station, where I barely managed to get an extra ticket from someone. The ticket office was closed, the tickets sold out. The hall was packed full with a Russian-speaking audience. Therefore the poet performed without a translator. That was the first time I heard how artistically he read his "Babi Yar,"[1] which was already famous at that time. I don't remember the rest of the poetry. Questions were asked after the reading. When someone asked whom he knew among the émigré poets, Yevtushenko quickly answered: Strannik (Pilgrim)[2] and Ivan Elagin.[3] The answer surprised many people. A Soviet poet might know about Strannik through his spiritual conversations on Voice of America. But Elagin?

Not so long ago, Elagin's daughter Lilya Matveeva told me that on that first American trip Yevtushenko tracked down her father in New York and they had a great binge in a New York restaurant; the Soviet poet

* (First published in *Novyi zhurnal* [*The New Review*], 2017, No. 287. Translated from the Russian by Sibelan Forrester especially for the *Schuylkill Valley Journal*)

showed up with some girl from Bogata. Elagin has some lines about that event in his grotesque poem "Diogenes Lived in His Barrel." "Rattling goblets dashingly,/ I drink festively by candlelight.//A wandering poet is with me,/A skirt-chaser and joker./A little girl from Bogota/Is laughing at our table." The same night the "poet-joker" recited a poem of Elagin's from memory:

> I do not know the bitterness of nostalgia.
> I'm pleased by someone else's country.
> Of all that I left so long ago in Russia
> What I miss is a Russian window.
>
> I recollect it down until the present,
> When it gets to be dark in my soul—
> A window with a big cross in the center,
> At eventide a blazing window.

Yevtushenko made the émigré poet unspeakably happy, since he had dreamed all his life of being heard *there*, in his homeland. He wrote: "My verses will go, ringing,/Down Nevsky and Sretenka./You'll run into me,/ Readers—my heirs." That is to say, if not now then at least in the future his verses would ring out in the cities of Russia. But after that first meeting with Yevtushenko Elagin joyfully told his friends: "They know my poems in Russia already now!"

The poets met more than once after that in New York and in Pittsburgh, where Elagin taught Russian literature at the University of Pittsburgh. Evtushenko tried to push the poetry of his émigré colleague into print in the Soviet press, but he succeeded in this only after Elagin's death early in the years of *glasnost*.

In 1991 the University of Pennsylvania in Philadelphia gave a grant to the "two most famous Russian poets" to give lectures on Russian literature. Especially for foreigners, the "most famous" then were still Yevtushenko and Voznesensky. In that order. Therefore Yevtushenko arrived first, bringing with him his wife and two little sons. The family settled comfortably in a splendid house, and the head of the family started his teaching activity with enormous success. The students were delighted by the "Russian lectures," which tended to attract a huge audience. They were even delighted by the broken but witty and lively English of the "Russian professor," who was not at all shy about his English grammar and his English "*pronons*"—on the contrary, he would play cleverly with this or that phrase or group of words. You would often see the tall figure of the poet on campus, in his colorful jackets and ties: "I don't teach modesty, it's not my specialty," as he said somewhere. But for some reason his jackets and ties irritated a lot of people. That "lot" were usually from the "Brodskist" camp (to borrow poet Naum Korzhavin's expression). Yevtushenko irritated them with more than just with his jackets and ties.

Yevgeny Aleksandrovich felt completely comfortable In Philadelphia, as he did almost everywhere on our planet. He regularly visited the "Nord-Eest" (Philadelphia's Brighton Beach) with its Russian stores and restaurants, read his work in cultural centers there, visited private homes, and he also read for American audiences in the most various places. I met him fairly often in the Philadelphia poetry center and at the home of the director of that center, which later closed. Here he was always surrounded by a flock of new friends and admirers. Later, already in the new millennium, the Philadelphia Reader (with capital letters), connoisseur of Yevtushenko's poetry and literary sponsor, Mark Averbukh, gave the poet a certificate accompanied by a thousand dollars. He did so in thanks for "Babi Yar," "The Bratsk Hydroelectric Dam," "The Heirs of Stalin," "The Window Opens on White Trees…" and other poems that had helped his generation to make sense of the time it had lived in. True to himself, Yevgeny Aleksandrovich immediately asked me about the financial position of the donor, and the poet accepted the gift only after I assured him that he would not be ruined if he gave away a thousand dollars. Now Averbukh's Philadelphia certificate is kept in the Yevtushenko Museum in Peredelkino.

Evtushenko is linked with Philadelphia by one other important event. In 1991, in the Philadelphia church of Saint Andrew the First-Called (erected by Russian sailors who built the legendary cruiser Varyag at the Philadelphia Naval Yard), Yevgeny Aleksandrovich married Maria Novikova. (They called her a nurse. "She's a doctor," her husband would correct them.) Until Philadelphia they had a civil marriage. About his marriage to Maria (Masha) the poet spoke with a line from his poem: "The last attempt to be happy…" You could say that this union, Yevtushenko's fourth, was happy, and it was the longest—from 1986 until the poet's death. "My guardian angel," Evgenii Aleksandrovich always said to me about his wife.

About whom and about what did this talented self-lover, life-lover, woman-lover, truth-lover, labor-lover write? ... About himself, of course, but at the same time also about worldwide conflicts and problems, getting involved, debating, standing up for his views in poems, essays and journalism, calling to thousands in stadiums, shouting, hurting his throat: "Citizens, listen to me!" And in various ways he proclaimed to the whole world, "Your immortality turns out to be mortal, Vladimir Ilyich [Lenin]." Until his last breath Yevtushenko was the conscience of his time; he endured deafening fame, such as no Russian poet had dreamed of.

And he endured just as deafening a fall. Things reached a point where an effigy of the poet, so recently famed and elevated, was burned on a Moscow street. "My soul was seared through with slander,/They lashed me with all kinds of rumors..." And that was no exaggeration. Perhaps it helped the poet that he was from Siberia? He wrote about that:

> I don't know what will happen with me.
> To keep my feet, not to go mad.
> But the lad from the train station lives in me—
> from the very warmest station—Zima[4]...

And moreover, perhaps, because the Lad from Zima station lived by his own rules, written into the lines of his poems, into the titles of his books... For instance: "There are no uninteresting people in the world..." Yes, he was always surrounded by all kinds of people—famous and ordinary, friends and foes, defenders and accusers. It's true, there seemed to be more of the latter, or they were noisier, because his friends and defenders often disappeared, went off to one side, when they should have taken the poet's side openly, in print. He wrote and spoke about that too. But his life was like that, he knew no other. And here's what else: "Don't die before your death." Oh, what a desire that was! And even in the final months and days of his life, how he strove with his last strength to follow those words. Far earlier, to celebrate his sixtieth birthday, Yevtushenko wrote a light, optimistic poem "There are no years" [in Russian, "Nyet lyet"]:

"There are
no years…"—
here's what the crickets creak to us to answer
our fears of aging
and drink dew until they're delirious,
hanging on stems aweigh,
and each—
is a miniscule little green poet.
There are
no years. […]
We all,
falling foolish into herd mentality
think up old age for ourselves,
but what kind of life is it
when it's a self-prohibition?

We, Yevtushenko's contemporaries, witnessed the way he, without
"self-prohibitions," and probably against the prohibitions of doctor
Masha, after his leg was amputated,[5] went on a reading tour with presen-
tations literally "from Moscow out to the very edges" (Moscow to Vlad-
ivostok). And until his last days he was working on a gigantic, multivol-
ume poetic Anthology… He lived by the word, as if there were no years,
nor illnesses, nor death!

I recall how once Yevgeny Aleksandrovich called me from Tulsa, where
he was teaching then, and said that he had written a poem about me. "I
want to read it to you. If you like it—I'll publish it." He read it. I liked
it, of course. He published this poem ("A Philadelphia Portrait") in his
collections.

For a while, two or three years it seems, we were out of touch. And when
what I would call a harsh and stupid persecution began, I felt very sorry
for the poet. I realized that no one was going to defend him from the
hurtful and ludicrous attacks, frequently cooked up out of envy of someone else's success. These literary intrigues and squabbles came from all
sides onto the internet—that marvel of our era, which covers the whole
world with an avalanche of important and useful information and, at the
same time, all kinds of unnecessary and harmful nonsense. A stupid con-

frontation suddenly appeared: "Brodsky versus Evtushenko." They were striking two completely different poets against each other.

Yevgeny Aleksandrovich, being a contemporary person (not like me), often wandered through the wilds of the internet. It was especially painful for him to confront hurtful words, composed by his former friends, directed at him. Unfortunately, the poet took these literary intrigues and gossip more seriously than his own serious illnesses. I wanted to help him somehow, in some way. But I understood that I had no way to help. What was needed was a literary figure with a name known in Russia and abroad, who would thunderously say, "Gentlemen, what are you doing?! Stop this harsh and unworthy game!" But Yevtushenko found no such defender. Yevgeny Aleksandrovich complained to me about the inertness of his friends and admirers. I tried to support him by quoting other statements about him—by worthy people who understood the significance of this Poet for Russian literature and for Russia itself. I told him more than once, "'Don't pay attention, maestro…'—just you spit on that whole evil chatter from the top of the highest tree!" I quoted Alexander Gladkov: "Yevtushenko is the medium through whom time speaks." And Shostakovich, who after the triumph of his Thirteenth Symphony to the words of Evtushenko (the Symphony's first section is called "Babi Yar"), wrote: "Upon closer acquaintance with this poet it became clear to me that he has a great talent, and most importantly a talent that *thinks*." I reminded him that the composer had thanked him for helping him express the problem of human conscience in music. "After all, Gladkov and Shostakovich don't say things like that about just anyone!" This helped a bit, but the poison was strong and continued to act.

In that time of troubles I would call the poet fairly often at his home in Tulsa, Oklahoma. He seemed to be glad when I called, otherwise our conversations would have been considerably shorter. After all, he was teaching, working intensively on his Anthology, and always writing poetry. In our conversations Yevgeny Aleksandrovich would talk about his day-to-day life in a remote part of America. For example, how he had wound up there. He was offered a teaching position at the university, and he set out to get acquainted with the unfamiliar city. He was on his way to the university when suddenly a clock on the square started to play "Lara's theme" from the movie *Doctor Zhivago*. The poet took this as a good sign. And he was not mistaken. Oklahoma was good to him. His classes at the university were huge, he even had to start capping the number of students: no more than 150 persons. Tulsa declared him an honorary citizen of the city. "All the members of my family are American citizens. But I will remain a subject of Russia until the end of my life," he said with pride. Many yards in Tulsa contain oilrigs: some lucky people in Oklahoma can pump oil from the depths and get rich. But the morals there are Puritan, a bit strange for a Russian poet with Don Juan tendencies. He told me about one amusing incident. A female student helped a male student in her class, who wanted to become a writer (influenced by the Russian professor?), to manage English grammar, on which he was a bit weak. At the end of class the future writer kissed her hand. The female student was offended by such audacity and complained to the administration. They began a detailed examination of the "case." They asked "the victim" which part of her hand was imprinted by the "criminal" kiss—above or below her wrist?

Once Yevtushenko told me that he meant to include the Russian poems of Shevchenko[6] in his Anthology. I told him that if he did both sides would be angry with him: Ukrainians because the Russkies would be "stealing" their national poet, and the Russkies because he was publishing Taras Hryhorovych in a Russian anthology. But I heard that all the same Shevchenko made it into the Anthology with his Russian poems. And it didn't start the Third World War. On that point: Yevtushenko was very concerned about Russia's conflict with Ukraine. He couldn't understand how two brotherly peoples were unable to live in peace! After all, two opposite systems had come together—capitalism and communism. And together they had vanquished fascism!

Yevgeny Yevtushenko was a marvelous interlocutor: intelligent, sensitive, resourceful; his statements and witty stories would stick in your memory. Perhaps he had already published some of his apt observations and utterances on this or that theme somewhere, but for me they were interesting and novel. For example, once he said, "Russia isn't as bad as the foreigners would like, but it's also not as good as we Russians wish it was." Once I asked him why he always began his letters of request (because Yevtushenko was always writing to someone on behalf of someone) in this way: "I, Yevgeny Yevtushenko, nominated x times for the Nobel Prize, the author of x books, a member of these and those organizations..."—since after all his name already said all that. He answered instantly, "I know. But I also know the people I'm writing to. It has an effect on them, and I want my requests to be granted." (I didn't ever ask about his jackets and ties; they weren't interesting to me.)

Yevtushenko never spoke about my poems. That was a sign, of course, that he didn't like them. Therefore I never once mentioned my own poetic production in our conversations. But not long ago he asked me for something for his Anthology. And then once again—not a sound. Yet the poet praised my essays, he tried fairly energetically to persuade me to write my autobiography and publish it in Russia, saying he would write a foreword. I thanked Yevgeny Aleksandrovich, but turned down his project: I wasn't interested in writing a book about myself, and besides it was already a bit late for that.

In almost every one of our conversations Yevgeny Aleksandrovich would declaim the verses of some poet, enthusiastic about this or that line in the poem. Most often he would recite from memory. Without such a phenomenal ability to love and even marvel at the lines of any other poet that had touched this sensitive and receptive reader (as Yevgeny Yevtushenko was until his last breath) in some way, his monumental book *Stanzas of the Century* would not exist.

I spoke with him for the last time three weeks or so before his death. He was at home. For the first time he was complaining a lot about his health, which he hadn't done even around the time his leg was amputated. To my question "Zhenya, what's wrong?" he answered, "I don't want to talk about it, they still need to do some tests." He criticized the movie *Tainstvennaya strast* (Mysterious Passion) with hurt feelings and bitterness: "They underrated me there, they lied, they distorted the facts. Friends came to see me at home, they were sympathetic. But once again no one with a name came out in print." And then, as in the past, he started reciting someone else's poems—in a weak voice, but with inspiration. He asked what was new with me. I said that while he had been away an interesting book had come out, *Poety v Nyu-Yorke* (*Poets in New York*, edited and compiled by Yakov Klots). "And is Irina Mashinski in the book?" After hearing an affirmative answer he said, "Good." I told Irina about that, she was excited and deeply touched.

And there in the telephone receiver came the last words Yevgeny Aleksandrovich ever addressed to me: "Valya, don't die before I do."

Rest in peace, dear Poet!

Notes

1 "Babi Yar"—a long poem describing the Nazi shooting of Jewish civilians outside Kiev during the Second World War—an event underplayed in the USSR, which made Evtushenko's poem an act of civic courage.

2 Strannik (Pilgrim) was the pseudonym of Archbishop Ioann of San Francisco, whose name in the world was Prince Dmitry Alekseyevich Shakhovskoy.

3 Ivan Elagin (pen name of Ivan Venediktovich Matveyev, 1918-1987)—a prominent Russian émigré poet in the United States.

4 Zima—the Russian word for winter, with obvious associations of cold.

5 In August 2013, in Tulsa, his right leg was amputated below the knee.

6 Taras Hryhorovych Shevchenko (1814-1861)—the most famous nineteenth-century Ukrainian poet.

FOREWORD

Flash fiction is *any* sudden story that functions on the strengths of its character(s), using particular images to convey action within a held moment. Over the past twenty years, flash fiction has made its mark. Depending on length, which can range from 100-2500 words; yet settles comfortably around 1000 words, flash fictions offer readers a glimpse into a pocket of life. Sometimes, flash fictions can contain a fully developed story arc, or has a single, significant action that sets the character(s) in reaction to that single event.

The stories selected for this issue of *Schylkill Valley Journal* were written by both established and emerging writers, using a wide variety of techniques and styles. What these stories share is the *flash*—that single moment where all things change, either implicitly or explicitly, by decisions made with or without thinking of the consequences—*il fait accompli.*

M.J. Iuppa
Flash Fiction Editor
Schuylkill Valley Journal

ROAD TRIP

by Cynthia Darling

New York was pushing in on me, and I told my boyfriend Steven so.

"I want to get out. Take a road trip. We've got to drive." I was living in Westchester, a place of SUVs and huge highways and a whole lotta not going anywhere. Steven said he'd take me up along the Hudson. I brought a map and snacks for the car: trail mix, Snapple diet iced tea, Twizzlers. Steven came to my house in his turquoise hatchback sports car, a compact little number that reminded me of the seventies. He had to fold himself in half to fit his 6'4" frame into the two-seater. Steven's scruffy blonde hair brushed the top of the car roof. He wore a blue ski vest and green sweater. My black wool coat was hot for the car, and I unbuttoned it, shedding its bulk. I was not as tall as Steven, but I still felt the sides of the car against me. We headed up route 9. As we drove, I put on lipstick using the passenger side mirror and combed my curly hair. The Hudson was grey blue, a sheen, on our left.

"I was picturing stopping in Croton-on-Hudson," Steven said, his British accent soft and alluring to me, even in these small conversations in the car.

"I like that," I said. The road stretched out in my mind's eye.

After twenty minutes, we were there.

"And there it is," Steven said happily. I sat silent. Where was the driving on to nowhere?

"I'm looking forward to a nice steak and potatoes," Steven said, rubbing his hands together in his way, half little boy, half British gentleman.

"Ok, let's wander through the town and see what we find."

"Actually, I've found a nice place already. It has five stars on Yelp. I'll just take us there."

After lunch, we walked out to the sidewalk. Brown rails and train cars and trestles and electric wiring met in a grand confluence. I liked the industrial oldness.

"Well, that was delicious," Steven said. "A nice nap is an order now."

"Let's go walk amongst the old rail tracks," I said, heading toward the metal stairs leading down.

"Oh, that doesn't look very safe," Steven said. I was stepping down two at a time, eager to get down there. I looked back. Steven stood at the top of the stairs.

"I'll just wait here for you, then."

I kept going. I hit the gravel and began meandering amongst the tracks. The different colors of rust and metal worked their magic on me, and soon I was snapping pictures of all of the different trains, some in operation, some not. The Hudson was barely visible through all the steel and metal. Then I was climbing back up again, Steven now sitting at the top of the stairs. He looked at me, his eyes soft and gentle. He reached his hand to my cheek and pulled me in to kiss me.

"Let's keep going up route 9," I murmured, as I settled on to his lap.

"It's time to go back. I'm going to nap and then do some work."

"Steven, remember? You wanted to take me? Out of Westchester?"

"Yes—this has been perfect. I want to take you to bed now." We stood up to go back to his turquoise sports car. We folded ourselves inside.

Back at his apartment, we walked inside and he pulled me and took me to his bed. We kissed and I felt myself giving in to his kind but insistent body. I was lost in the press of his hips, my hands grasping the muscles of his chest, the edge, the edge, that I went to. Afterwards, we lay in his white down comforter. He brought me tea, milky and sweet the way he liked it. Steven was kind. And he was sexy. And he would keep on folding himself into that turquoise sports car and checking Yelp for as long as I knew him. I saw many dates of even-keeled, moderate jaunts to places not that far away. But our love, here, in this bed, was the place that would take me to where I didn't know I was going.

THE NEW LIEUTENANT

by Allen X. Davis

What's that on the road up ahead? asked the new lieutenant as their jeep approached the center of the small dusty village. It's a body sir, answered the driver. It was lying in the morning sun like a pile of dirty laundry. Probably an enemy collaborator left there as a warning, sir. Villagers went about their business as if it wasn't there. Slow down, said the lieutenant when they were almost up to it. He took out his camera and snapped pictures as they inched along in slow motion. He was fresh out of college and yearned to be back on campus where the future looked bright, but now he was like a snake shedding its skin, never to wear the old skin again. The driver tried not to look but it happened quick like a snapshot. The body was barefoot and gray and he saw himself walking barefoot on the beach back home, his feet squishing into the wet, gray— Okay, let's go, ordered the LT. At the next village lay another body. The lieutenant did not take out his camera. They did not stop.

PACKY & BACKY

by Allen X. Davis

You should be *ashamed* of yourself, complains the woman in the back seat to her husband-boyfriend. Doing something like that to a fifty-year-old woman. Her eyes are hidden behind dark sunglasses and you think bruises and black eyes yet she seems to be grinning ever so slightly. You're taking them to the package store for more booze, then back home —their third packy & backy in two days. Hey, he declares, staring straight ahead, I told you nine fuckin' times to shut your fuckin' pie hole, but would you listen? Noooo. It's your own damn fault. And besides, you're only forty-eight. He's kind of a big dude in a black shirt buttoned all the way up to the neck like a priest. With you I feel like I'm sixty, she snaps back. Hey driver, smiles the dude, would you let a woman talk to you like that? My ex-wife said she was going to kill me and then kill herself, you answer. But of course the judge didn't care. See, she says, you should consider yourself lucky. Lucky, he mutters, staring straight ahead again as if in deep thought. Last week when we made this same packy run her brother rode along, fresh out of prison that very morning. He had a few drinks in him but sat there fairly quietly in a work jacket looking out the window while the other two, half drunk, bounced off the walls. Turn that up! shouted the dude when Bob Seger came on the radio and all three of them sang along to Night Moves. You wonder where the brother is today—hopefully not back in prison but working and getting his shit together, unlike these two. She's havin' hot flashes, says the dude when we pull up to Kappy's Liquors. We gotta get somethin' to cool her off! She comes out of the packy holding a single rose, slightly wilted. He loves me! she cries, and sticks it in her hair. And he's sorry for what he did. Shhh! he hisses. I know, she sighs, I know. She leans over, whispers something to him and explodes into laughter—shrieks and shrieks of wild, derisive laughter—while he sits there, smaller than before.

THE PHIAL

by Melody Smith

Cigarette smoke filled the front seat of the old ford as Aaron sped around a large eight-wheeler. It honked loudly, and he sighed, knowing that he had been on the road for eight hours too many without taking a break. He pulled over onto the next exit, the green and white highway sign barely visible in the moonless night, and rubbed his tired eyes. He knew he still had a solid four or five hours left, but unless he wanted to become the next tragic news story, getting some rest might be a good idea.

As soon as he had begun to close his eyes, a roaring horn blasted again, startling him awake.

"Still too close to the highway for some actual sleep I guess," he muttered, starting his truck up "understood LOUD and clear." His rusted truck pulled away from the gas station where he had stopped briefly and made its way through the small nowheresville town. Quickly, however, Aaron realized that his need for sleep might have to hold off for a little bit since, seemingly out of nowhere, a thick fog had snuck up, engulfing his truck and all but the brightest lamp lights hanging overhead.

He cursed under his breath, straining his eyes for somewhere to pull over that wasn't accidently someone's yard or the middle of the road—HA! He spied in the distance some bright blinking neon sign: 'A Fine Kettle of Fish' is what it was supposed to read but, at this distance with the fog (and the fact that the place had clearly seen better day since numerous letters were dimmed or out completely) it simply read 'Kettle.' He backed in to the lot and instantly fell asleep, tattered overcoat wrapped tight around his body like a shroud. Dreams of watery fog replaced by rushing currents and never-ending cliff side rails swelled within, lulling him to slumber.

Only to be woken up minutes later by a loud pounding on his door. Aaron grunted and turned away, but the persistent knocking wouldn't stop, just kept getting louder and louder. He pushed himself up and found himself staring directly in the eyes of some lanky college kid, who looked extremely put out at having to wait so long. He was mouthing something… Aaron could vaguely tell—his own eyes still bleary from exhaustion, and now the young man was... gesturing? At the window? It was hard to see his own reflection in the fog, nonetheless another person.

As soon as he cranked down the window, the young man instantly started yelling loudly about company policy and trespassing.

"—And if you don't buy something, then like, we are going to have to TOTALLY kick you out and call the cops and that is way too much work for all of us, I mean like C'MON MAN!" the young man finished out of breath, and pointed forcefully at him and then back towards the Kettle.

"Uh," Aaron said, "I mean, sure, if I have to I guess I can… buy a cup of coffee, or something?" With that, he opened the truck door, and followed the man into the Kettle.

The Kettle was dimly lit, and the smell of mold was only rivaled by the smell of frying fish with a subtle hint of sulfur under everything else. A stage, old and out of repair, stood to the side, with what Aaron could only presume was some local comedian who didn't have a lot going on in his comedy or life, judging by the bored stares from the few patrons dispersed amongst the open tables. The bar, however, was in much better condition; worn but shining and well stocked, the bartender idly cleaning glasses as he shook his head despairingly at the comedian at the stage. Aaron took a seat at the bar, stool shrieking as he settled.

Before he could even order anything, the man from before loudly proclaimed to the bartender to get him a coffee, before stomping away to the side in a huff. The bartender chuckled. "Sorry about him, he's the owner's son. Gotta put up with him, y'know?" he said, fetching a mug of coffee from the back for him.

Aaron sat idly, the crackling sound of static-filled radio only serving to tempt him back to sleep. A shriek of the stool next to him shook him out of that, and he turned his head at the intrusion. It was a young woman, short-cropped blonde hair with black roots showing through. She looked like she was wearing at least three different coats—a vest, jacket, and winter coat all visible and straining against each other.

"Oh, I didn't mean to wake you—you look like you've had a bit too much to drink, huh?" she smirked a little. "Name's Lynn—what's yours, Stranger?"

"Aaron." He pushed himself up onto his elbows, a small headache starting to form in his right temple. As he was sitting up, the bartender pushed him a small blue mug of coffee and nodded at him before going back to cleaning glasses. Lynn didn't seem to talk to the bartender or even notice him, continuing to stare at Aaron like he was a puzzle to solve.

It should have made his skin crawl, he hated people staring at him; but surprisingly, it didn't.

"So what are you doing here? I mean, you're obviously not from around here—are you?" she asked, raising an eyebrow.

"Yeah—no. I'm just passing through. I got caught in the fog and needed a place to pull over before heading back out and driving in this mess. Catch a few z's for a while if I could." At the mention of driving, Lynn's face slit into a grin and Aaron heard the bartender groan quietly behind them.

"Lynn, c'mon don't do this to every stranger that comes in here," The bartender said, fixing a glare at her. Lynn just tilted back her head and laughed.

"Ignore him." She was still laughing lightly. "He's full of bull and he knows it."

"Don't do what?" Aaron asked, uneasiness settling in like an old friend.

She fixed him with a piercing gaze. "You aren't from around here right? And you got a car?"

The uneasiness was building bit by bit.

"…Yes? What of it?"

Lynn clapped her hands together in a quick, startling motion, causing Aaron's eyes to bulge open.

"It's settled then! You'll take me out of this shithole and drop me off at the first good city that comes our way, and I'll provide you quality roadside commentary, you won't know what hit you!"

Aaron was shocked and a bit weirded out. He'd never seen such a forward person outside some of the criminals he helped put away when he was a cop. Well, that and… The Girl. Aaron fixed a bewildered stare at the odd woman before he started to chuckle, that turned into a full-blown belly laugh.

The waiter from before turned his way and made a disgusted noise, before strutting into the kitchen, but Aaron didn't notice. This woman, Lynn, was so much like her that it was ridiculous. Lynn was tall and brash—The Girl was tall and brash. Lynn had miserably dyed hair—The Girl had miserably died hair, although hers was a terrible shade of green. Aaron wiped his eyes, bizarre and sudden mirth dying down after a minute.

Lynn was staring at him like he was crazy.

"Sorry," Aaron said, coughing up into his hand in an attempt to save face "I—you. You just reminded me a whole hell of a lot like someone I used to know."

She relaxed, eyes no longer popping out of her head in surprise. "It's all right, I guess. A bit odd, but hey! Better than you saying no to my proposal?"

"Your propo— oh that." Aaron's mind racing, still not able to get the image of The Girl, *Cindy,* out of his head. He didn't hear her when Lynn repeated the question; he suddenly immersed in memory he was trying to forget.

A tiny girl on a swing set, being pushed higher and higher until she tumbled into the sky. A man in an overcoat was rushing to catch her but he missed, her scraped knees and wails filling the empty playground.

A small girl with pink-and-green-and-yellow flower backpack nervously clinging onto his leg on the second day of school, her mother not able to be there with her. The man ruffled her hair and with a gentle shove, pushed her towards the school, instantly sending her into an excited run towards the building.

A girl ranting to him about her parents not caring about her boyfriend, she was in LOVE and how couldn't they just SEE THAT! as he made two cups of coffee, one black and one filled to the brim with sugar.

An older girl nervously fixing her collar, her first big interview is today. The man steps in and fixes it and squeezes her shoulder. They enter an old rusted truck and drive off to her interview. Both are disappointed her father couldn't join her.

A young woman throws a square tasseled hat up, holding a yellow and white diploma and the man rushed over, hugging her tight and quick, before she embarrassedly pushed him away to have someone take their photo. They go to dinner together the two of them later that night, just the two of them, and he tries not to cry with pride.

A woman is sitting at his coffee table, angrily pushing clothes into a duffel bag as she yells, the man yelling back. A picture frame of a man and a woman falls off the wall as he punches it, knuckles bruised and bleeding. The man stops, parental worry entering his eyes, but before he can offer to helps, she's sprinting out the door duffle bag in one hand, keys in the other, shrieking about false fathers and liars…

Aaron is pulled out of the sudden onslaught of memories just as he saw a car crash, a funeral, a body burning into nothing but a small phial filled with dark ash. He shakes himself and looks up.

"I *said*," her tone almost taking on an annoyed quality, "are you going to take me out of here, or what?"

The bartender and Lynn stare at him. He thumbs the small phial in his pocket, toying idly with the rubber stopper for a few moments.

"In the morning, I haven't slept in what seems like forever." The bartender and Lynn's jolt at that, obviously surprised by his answer, before the bartender begrudgingly hands over a twenty-dollar bill to Lynn's outstretched hand.

She shrugs jerking a thumb at the bartender, "He always thought I could never leave this place. Where are you headed anyway? I mean—I don't really care but most people don't drive through-who-knows-where-Pennsylvania without a reason, especially not in this fog."

"Niagara Falls." Aarons answers sharply.

"Niagara Falls? You going on vacation or something?" Lynn asked, noticing the small phial in his hand.

"… No just…" He holds the phial in his hand, remembering years ago, planning a trip with Cindy for her 21st birthday there. See the Falls, cross the border and hit up a few casinos, share a beer with her, laugh and smile and love—

"… Business." He finishes lamely, quickly but gently lets go of the phial in his pocket, before downing the rest of his coffee. He shouldn't have. He needs to sleep, but even with the coffee in his system he's tired enough that it shouldn't be a problem. He's been this tired for a long while now, after all.

She eyes him curiously. "Huh. Well a vacation would be better, but to each their own, I suppose. I'm gonna take the cot in the back room, I'll see you in the morning before I leave, okay?"

"'Kay Lynn," the bartender says, prying the mug away from Aaron, who is quickly starting to slump onto the table.

The next morning the fog is gone, but it's still wet, pouring buckets straight down in a harsh cascade of water upon them, like a gorge flooding. Aaron gets the truck running and Lynn fills his glove box with old cassette tapes, fitting nice nicely next to his old gun and a picture of his retirement party from the station. She doesn't even bat an eye at the gun, simply staring out the window with a wide smile on her face.

Aaron huffs out a small laugh and turns the key in ignition; the old truck sputters to life, and glides out of the Kettle parking lot, into the gray downpour of a new morning.

GREY HUE

by Salvatore Difalco

~after Thomas Bernhard's wicked miniatures

Due largely to my appearance—an over-sized head, large black liquid eyes, thin lips and tiny nose—people often assign to me extraterrestrial origins. Far from being offended, I'm amused, and continue to be amused when people make that assignation. I was born on this planet, rest be assured, and inherited my looks directly from human parents. My mother had a large bulbous skull, despite being very petite. She also had an enormous brain and a PhD in molecular biology. My father, a statistician, had the big, lambent eyes. He was Hungarian. My mother often said he hypnotized her with those eyes. And I've found, in my strange walk through life, that I can also hypnotize women. That is to say, I've never lacked for dates, lovers and long-term squeezes. I've had a normal—perhaps even robust—sex life, despite my odd looks.

I like my looks. The capacious skull speaks of my intelligence. And my bottomless eyes absorb every detail of the world like black holes absorb matter and energy. My curiosity for the world is boundless. And my thin lips and tiny nose convey to all the delicacy of my physical and moral constitutions. I speak quietly but precisely. I never sneer at others, for I cannot sneer. I walk around my city with an open mind and open heart. If some choose to mock my appearance, I pity them, for they must surely hate themselves and their own flawed humanity in order to point the finger at me and suggest I come from another planet. And were that true, would you not be curious to know what life is like up there? Would you not wish to know why I am visiting? Would you not wish to know about my technologies?

Humans are silly creatures, when all is said and done. Our pettiness, our primitivism would likely put off any visiting aliens. Perhaps they'd incinerate us. When a group of lads standing at a corner accost me with references to E.T. and The Thing, I am not offended in the least. I face the lads and tell them this: Do you think that if I was a real alien I would hesitate for one second blasting you off the face of the earth, you pusillanimous little scumbags? They are surprised by my outburst, taken aback by my confidence, and alarmed by the long thin finger I point at them.

SURROUNDED BY THE CORN

by Ray Greenblatt

I didn't notice at first. The house was low, cozy, with a picture window in front. Just big enough for me.

A small living room with stone fireplace. A dining room. I did not dine anymore. I put the leaves in the dining room table to use for sewing. It filled the room.

A small bedroom. Another room that most would use as a second bedroom. I saw a delightful extravagance there. I'd throw in there what I did not use at once. Although I didn't save much anymore. An extravagant closet.

From the small kitchen, I could mix a drink and walk out the back door to the lawn chairs. Sit and swish the cubes. Inhale and let the smoke slide out. All slow, quiet. But I didn't notice the corn growing.

Moving in in the spring threw me off. Gave me no hint. I wasn't prepared to get ready.

In the cold spring, I could see in all directions. I could see the fields stretched north to the mountains. West to the woods. East to a neighboring farm.

But now the corn was growing. Growing higher. Weaving into a curtain. Thick green.

In the spring, the ground was simply dirt. Rutted with slivers of frost in the ruts. Only the roots of dead corn left from the previous season. I had forgotten it would grow.

I couldn't sit on the back lawn much longer. I couldn't see. Funny how I couldn't sit with Robert either. That was boredom. A tangible state. For a salesman he had nothing to say to me anymore. But this should be far simpler. The corn was blocking my view. And, yet, it was more complicated. What could I do?

I would stay in the house and sew. Sew for my grandchildren whom I didn't see anymore. My children should not feel sorry for me. I was rid of Robert and his demands. But I couldn't tell them that.

Write to old friends. But they knew Robert. The grown child who was not mine but called on me one day. Another of Robert's peccadilloes. And she wanted money.

It was hot in the house. I would sew. If I turned on the fan, the patterns would blow.

Symphonies were cold. Like light on a distant planet. Popular music brought back events like stones on my head.

I couldn't find what I wanted. The right book? Stories, memoirs, poems were all memories I could do without.

Cleaning was a past livelihood I would never do again. It wasn't for Robert. It was after Robert's guests had left. The ones he wouldn't tell me about, but just bring home. I rid myself of their remains.

And the corn is still growing. At dusk, it rustles like old voices. I'll build myself a fire in the fireplace. It's so hot. I must do something. Mix my smoke with the fire's.

They say whiskey heats you up. It cools my insides. Keeps me dancing balanced.

I look out the picture window. I can't go out. Several cars pass by. I must duck so they can't see me.

The veins in my breasts are pulsing, as if ink were injected under the skin. So many meandering tributaries. There are hairs in my navel. I touch that membrane between my legs. An old reminder.

Rough below my knees. Funny. Like husks of corn.

I am sexless now. Like I want to be. Like I fought Robert to be. I look down at myself as if I were a slab hanging from the ceiling. Touch my graying hair like unruly weeds that should be pulled.

The tide of corn has boxed me in. I'm sure some things will come out of the corn one night. It howls with burning throat. Sucks in the moon. Flings out the light.

I'll search through the cellar for something the last owners left. Maybe they'll give me something, something to do.

The corn has given me the only way out. The cars go by faster. The traffic speeds up. There is just a blur of time roaring past my picture window. That could suck me into its stream, its timelessness.

HORSIE

by Dick Bentley

Glenda looks up suddenly. Charlie is dragging a toy automobile across the kitchen floor.

"It won't work," Charlie says.

"Here, let me see it," Glenda says. Charlie seems on the verge of tears. Glenda studies the car, partly constructed from Legos. She twists a small plastic piece that shows the car's wheels.

"There, now it will work."

"No, it won't," Charlie says.

Glenda puts the car on the floor, points at it, rolls it back and forth, and lets it go. It leaps across the room and crashes into the refrigerator. Charlie goes over and nudges it with his foot.

"Do you want to play with it?" Glenda asks.

"No," says Charlie.

"Then pick it up and put it away."

He doesn't move.

"Put it away," she says, coming toward him one step at a time, "or I will eat you."

Charlie runs for the stairs shrieking. The dog begins to bark.

"Look, Charlie," Glenda says, "you are impossible. You've spilled the groceries, you've kicked over the dog's water. Look at this mess. Let's go outside and play a game." She reaches for his hand, which he pulls away.

"I'll be your pony," she says. "Come, Charlie."

Outside, Glenda kneels down. She thumps her hands on the grass and neighs. She moves her body up and down.

"Come," she says. "Your pony is waiting."

Charlie squats down and throws a leg over her back. He smiles as she bumps him up and down, while he holds onto her sweater.

Up on the second floor, Ellen watches Charlie and Glenda as they play on the grass. She is alarmed, and comes rushing down the stairs, and out the front door. "Glenda," she cries out. "Stop this at once."

"Your father is enjoying this," Glenda says. "I'm sorry, but all this is hard work."

"Dad," Ellen cries, "get off of Glenda. If you keep this up, we'll have to send you to the nursing home." She turns to Glenda, "As for you, young lady, I have never seen such behavior. This goes beyond normal caregiving."

Charlie looks up at Ellen, his daughter. "She's just being nice," he tells her. "She's just being nice, like your Mama used to be."

He looks down at Glenda.

"Giddyup horsie," he says.

THROUGH THE KEYHOLE
an addict's account
by Rob Kaniuk

Part 1

The Ukrainian called with news. He got the big settlement we'd been waiting for. This would keep us satisfied for a while. We both owed money around town to dealers, and had no credit left to speak of. All of our usual schemes of scrapping copper, and pawning gently borrowed items had been exhausted. The thoughts of how to score were getting darker every day.

"Can you find anything?" he asked.

"I can make some calls, how many?"

There is always an understanding between addicts: If I could find something, you had to share it with me—on a percentage basis, respective of quantity and risk. I felt like I hit the junkie jackpot when he told me, "Get what you can for a thousand—we're getting as high as a giraffe's asshole tonight!" I called around to see who had the best price on bulk, and was less than excited to find that I'd have to deal with Johnny Finch.

Two things are held close to the chest in this situation. Never tell the end user what the price per unit is—to keep the skim as heavy as possible, and never, under any circumstances, disclose who the connection is. "I'll take care of you," wasn't always in exact proportion of the legwork. This way I was sure my services were needed, and that I'd get mine.

A purchase this big was always dangerous. Both sides paranoid that the other was going to rob them. There were usually weapons, bag men, and plenty of time to plan it out. However, I needed a broker to bring it together quickly and without incident—someone familiar to both parties.

Johnny was the guy, and would receive a cut of the final haul. This kid was shifty as a squirrel hiding a nut, and about as sharp as a bag of wet mice. But the true value of our type, junkie to junkie, was in our connections. Johnny had proven his worth in the past with rock solid connections, even in periods of countywide drought.

But I knew him too well. We were the same at the core. There was a silent but understood jockeying between us, trying to fuck the other over and always looking for the next junkie stunt. Not too much though, you never knew when you'd need a favor.

I left in a fever to grab the cash from The Ukrainian, picked up Johnny, and he directed me toward what used to be the heartbeat of Delaware County—the Port of Chester.

I asked all of the relevant questions on the ride there: "How well do you know this guy? How often do you deal with him? What is the final price per unit? How long will the deal take?"

Johnny assured me it was all good. "I've dealt with this guy a bunch, he's cool, always a good deal on quantity, you'll be real happy with it— trust me." He looked away with the last part of that statement, and it was that last part that worried me.

Finch knew I didn't trust him, none of us trusted one another. We were desperate addicts who have stolen from our own family members. We couldn't be trusted.

But it wasn't my money I was putting up. What did I care if we got a discount?

Johnny was even more removed from The Ukrainians cash than I was, and he was salivating at the prospect of some free shit. His hope for this deal to go through wouldn't allow him to voice the doubts he had. The Ukrainian, Finch, and I had one thing in mind, and no risk was ever assessed in our state of wanting. We saw the world through the keyhole of an ink dark room.

This life is one filled with gambles but the addict rarely thinks of what is really at stake—am I about to get burnt? Will I get caught? Will I be arrested? Will I make it out of this alive? Will she leave me when she finds out?

We just push further to the edge with every gamble, and experience each losing hand as a run of bad luck—as if shit decisions didn't create shit luck. At the end of the day, there was always someone else to blame.

A MAJOR DRUG-HUB since the 80's, Chester seemed a likely place to go for a buy of this magnitude. The pseudo-city had never recovered after the jobs left in the 60's. Instead of the shipyards and auto plants of the past—the main export in this—the asshole of Pennsylvania—was now pain and suffering. The atmosphere in this waterfront town reeked of desperation, proving the motto on the welcome sign relevant as ever. "Welcome to Chester: What Chester makes, makes Chester."

I blasted past the sign in the blue Toyota pickup, laden with trash bags full of aluminum cans clinking around—my last hope for getting high today before the call came in.

Johnny was directed by phone to meet the guy on a side street. I parked in the only available spot, against traffic. It was hot and the air stagnant. There were people everywhere, searching for even the slightest breeze. Old folks filled porches trying to escape the stale air of their cramped row homes.

These people didn't like what their town had become, but had no means to escape it. Johnny and I were just part of the problem—two junkies, funding the demise of a people. Eyes on this crowded street stuck to me like my t-shirt doused in sweat. I couldn't shake them. Everywhere I looked, I was burned with another scornful glare.

I could feel the disgust they had for me. For what they had to deal with. For what they had to do to survive this town. Part of the hate I felt clinging to me was my own. I wanted to run, but couldn't see the path in front of me. I couldn't find a way through the keyhole, and back into the world.

Usually I would come up with something to keep me busy. Pop the hood of the car, feigning engine trouble. Get out some paperwork and pretend to read it while on the phone. Anything to look like I had a reason to stop where I did.

Waiting is just part of any drug transaction, so I learned to get used to it. It is the most vulnerable part of the deal. Just sitting alone with no excuse to be there. Given a location and time, you wait. And wait. And fucking wait—out of place in the wrong end of town. Like the Lou Reed song—Waiting for My Man.

This is why it's a good idea to come up with a decent location, where you don't look out of place if you're there for a while. Cause like Lou said, "he's never early, he's always late, first thing you learn is that you always got to wait." Some spots, you're just out of place no matter what charade is given. This was one of them.

Palms sweating and a knee bouncing from an involuntary foot tremor, I did what any good addict would: I sparked a bowl—to calm the nerves a bit. It worked for about three whole minutes, then the smell lingered around the truck and caused even more paranoia.

"Call this dude and find out where the fuck he is."

Johnny did—there was no answer.

"Text him then, we've been waiting too long. We look shady as shit just sitting here, Finch!"

He did. Still nothing.

After thirty minutes of radio silence and restless natives, Johnny's phone buzzed with a text message. *Be there in 5*

I took it to mean that he'd be there in ten or fifteen minutes, but was surprised when the phone rang in five minutes time. Johnny put the phone to his ear and said, "blue Toyota truck."

THINGS WENT FROM being tense to jovial in a matter of seconds. The withdrawal symptoms were beginning to lift, just at the thought of this deal coming to fruition.

When in wait, the vibration of a cell phone feels more like when the dice leave the hand at the craps table. Butterflies fill the belly, and a sense of hope fills your entire being. Is it the man? Is my long wait over? Will my lust for another hit be satisfied? This was all felt in the time it takes to lift the phone to see who it was.

It seemed that sometimes the whole ceremony of procurement was just as satisfying as using the actual drugs.

As he approached, my gut told me something was off. He was sweating profusely and panting as if he gimped here from Wilmington. This bastard looked like he hadn't walked for anything but to stuff his fat face in years. Patting his forehead with a dingy rag, dressed in tattered sweats, and hobbling around like a lame diabetic—this was not the picture of a successful drug dealer at all.

I was used to dealing with the kind of people who spent their profits on nice cars, and gold teeth. At the very least they had a shitty car with a good stereo system, and nice clothes. I paid good money to furnish these Chester "start-ups" with certain luxuries.

This asshole was on foot, in cutoff sweatpants. He lacked the standard issue I am used to seeing. He looked more like a vagrant I'd give a cigarette to on the street.

I imagined he still thought of a Craftmatic Adjustable bed as the pinnacle of high living, and that Wilford Brimley was doing God's work with those adverts. And he saw those ads, sitting on his greasy couch all damn day. I had instant disdain for this lousy mooch.

Fuck it, I thought, I hated most of my dealers anyway. Let's get it over with, before he collapses of heat stroke out here.

Johnny did something next which still makes me want to punch my own face—the gimp said, "Give me the money, I have to go grab them."

And this simple bastard handed a thousand dollars out the window.
I lost my shit.

"What the fuck are you doing, Finch? Go with him!"

"He's cool, trust me." He responded, offended at my outrage.

There it was again, trust me.

I've been burned before, and I knew at this point I'd probably never see the drugs or that sweat-soaked, diabetic gimp again. But the drug fiend has a wildly unrealistic amount of hope when it comes to the score. If there was a chance at getting some shit, we'd be there. If you were holding and your house was engulfed in flames, we'd be there to help put it out. Then politely ask for a hit—you know, for helping. There was never a scam too risky, or calamity too great, that would keep us from the pursuit.

Hope was a drug all its own, with an equally horrific crash when it was shorted. This was the nature of my kind. We dealt in synthetic feelings, and the hope for more. It's a gambler's life, and the hustle takes tremendous commitment.

In reality, nothing short of death would satisfy the urge, no matter how full the coffers—there was always a deal in the making.

I was raised with good morals, and bad habits. It took a while, but the bad habits had cast a shadow so large, that the morals and values I had once known, were all but lost. Gone was the boy filled with curious hope for the future. Nothing mattered. Just the score. Just the warped view, through the keyhole.

I had to give it to the man in the tattered sweats. He was well practiced in the art of the grift—after taking the cash, he called the police to report two white males smoking marijuana in a blue Toyota.

THE COPS ARRIVED, FURIOUS. They had been pulled from the scene of a homicide to deal with the nuisance of a pair of junkies.

"Get out of the truck, assholes. You just ruined my day, and you can bet you'll both be going to jail"

The cops were even more furious to only find a half gram of pot in the truck—but still enough to send us to jail. I managed to send a text to The Ukrainian from the back of the cruiser. *arrested—on way to jail*

It was a thing of genius by the grifter. With Johnny and me in cuffs, we couldn't give chase to a man who could barely walk in the first place.

I could imagine him sweating himself to death, in a frenzy of laughter, as he counted the stack of bills.

I was 4 years into a 5 year probation out of the state of Arizona when I was arrested. If they found out at booking, it meant that I couldn't bail out until Arizona was contacted, and their disposition was declared on the matter.

Would I have to go back to Arizona for a potential 9 year sentence (per the terms of my probation), or would they be lenient and release me to my supervising Probation Officer?

BOOKED INTO CHESTER, desperation was getting worse by the minute. The hours went by slowly, but the cell got crowded fast. The air conditioning was on full tilt to combat the stifling heat outside—the cinder block cell was freezing cold. I made a pillow of my shoes, and curled my knees into my t-shirt to stay warm.

Part 2

(Four years prior) Yavapai County, Arizona

I wake on a bunk, in a room with another man. The cell is 120 inches long, 78 inches wide. It is cold, filthy—I am dope-sick behind bars.

As the morning headcount commenced in the Yavapai County Detention Center, I looked out the thin sliver of a window above my concrete bunk.

It was the peaceful time of day in here, just as the sun shone against the sky prior to rising—right before the cacophonous bellow of my peers ensued. This came to be my 5 minutes of peace every morning.

Transfixed with an early sky—broad strokes in red and orange of every shade, inlaid with thin ribbons of purple, pink, and silver. Stark land specked with ornery and rugged plants defying arid soil, like the pockmarks of a face that has known a lifetime of suffering.

I sat for a while in this solitude and thought; "How the hell did I end up here?"

I was spending my honeymoon behind bars, trying to secure my release. One minor detail—I needed the sum of $25,000 cash to post bond.

AFTER LIVING and growing pot in a California compound for the previous 18 months, I came to Arizona intending to pass through.

At the end of my time in California, I was getting my shit together to head back east. Betty was flying out to meet me in San Fran, so we could spend a few days in the city for her birthday. Then we would head to Vegas to make an honest woman of her.

Red and Harlan were ready to leave the Mendocino compound for Lincoln, Nebraska. I had helped them get a job with us a few months before the harvest. I knew Red from back east. He had spent all of his money limping his busted-ass van from Philly to Garberville, CA to take part in the modern gold rush—almost legal weed. That van made it, but wouldn't take Red another mile. He pushed it into an alley behind the place he found work, and it would serve as his home for the next eight months.

Red met Harlan washing dishes at the Gypsy Rose Cafe and before long Red had himself a van-mate. Harlan was just glad not to be on the streets any longer and Red was happy to help. They were different cheeks of the same ass—acting like they'd known each other for years. The boys had experience in making high quality hash from the waste produced during harvest.

Through connections I made in my time there, I was able to keep them both busy making hash for some east coast transplants. When it was time to part, these butt buddies owed me a little cash for the startup costs. It wasn't much money and I wasn't looking for any extra, but they had something else in mind. A little thank you for getting them out of the van.

This gesture of kindness came by way of a leftover batch of hash that didn't make weight. The guys had a light brick of 308 grams, stamped with the word "california" from the custom press that I had built from an old license plate, some 2x4's, and a car jack. A pound weighs 454 grams—only whole pounds were agreed to be purchased by the buyer in Lincoln and it wasn't worth their risk to bring back anything but cash.

I was glad to take the brick with me, it would fetch 5-10 times what they owed me once I had it back in Philly. Besides, it was not like I had to bring a burlap sack full of pot back east—this was 8"x3"x2" in size. Very manageable.

We had a less than charming big rig driver with a toothless smile and an overall unkempt appearance named Hamburger Hank. He brought hundreds of pounds back east on a flatbed trailer disguised as an equipment hauler. I didn't have to worry about such a reasonable package as mine, in comparison.

I left the fog-banked hollers of northern Mendocino County and made my way to San Francisco. The plan was to pick up Betty at the airport around 3pm, but I had to stop and see Moog first.

TURK AND LEAVENWORTH—deep in the Tenderloin district of San Francisco—was where I first met Moog. If you were looking for drugs or a venereal disease, this was the spot to go. Open air sales, up and down the block. Cars double-parked with fiends being served at their window. Dealers lined the sidewalks, shouting what brand of oblivion they had to offer—all within sight of the local precinct. I'm not sure if it was tolerance by the bulls or arrogance by the dealers, but there was never any police intervention. It was like there were two blocks surrendered to the city's affliction—close enough to the cop shop to be considered a safe place to score. The traffic never stopped. And it was faster than the drive-thru at in-and-out.

Moog saw me make a buy and whispered out of the side of his mouth to follow him. I turned to see a white man who looked at home in the dark side of town. He was dressed in an impeccably matched sweatsuit, wearing gold rimmed sunglasses and gold Figaro chain. He looked like fat Elvis dragging a three-legged pit bull by the collar—intrigue alone made me follow. He brought me to his surprisingly well-kept second floor apartment around the corner. It felt much safer than dealing with the dregs of Turk and Leavenworth.

I detoured from my route to the airport, met Moog and made as big a buy as he could accommodate. Then I went to scoop up Betty. She was there waiting. I was so glad to see her. It had been too long.

My tour was over. It was great to finally be in each other's company. If absence makes the heart grow fonder, loneliness and misery made my heart cry for a familiar touch. We checked into a hotel on the Wharf and headed out on the town.

After a few days in the Golden Gate city, it was time to hit the road. The night before we left for Vegas, I contacted Moog for some road drugs. He said it was safe to stop by and I told Betty that I had to drop something off to my friend in the city before we left town. She knew I sold drugs, so it didn't seem out of the ordinary. Betty was just glad to think that I was getting rid of whatever I had brought from up north.

Betty was a good girl from a farm-town in central Illinois and hadn't known anything of the life I was living. Even the way we met was steeped in mystery to her. The secretive life was something of a novelty to this point, but she didn't want any parts of dealing drugs, let alone smuggling hash across the country.

WITH BETTY ASLEEP in the hotel, I went to meet Moog around midnight as we had planned. There was a little trouble finding his apartment. I never met him at night before, and it was a different world after dark. After crisscrossing the entire Tenderloin, I got nervous that I'd have to give up the mission and make the trip across our nation without the proper rations. Dope-sick and wild mood swings was not part of the honeymoon brochure I had presented to Betty. At this point, my body needed drugs just to get out of bed and combat sickness.

I began to panic. Moog wasn't answering the phone.

This is before everyone had a GPS on their smartphone, and could simply type in the address. I didn't even have an address to look for. Siri, take me to my drug dealer's house, in the tenderloin. That wasn't an option.

Finding my bearings, I finally made it to the apartment. I rang the bell and waited.

A gravelly voice came over the intercom, "Yo, who dis?"

"It's Rob—from Philly. You said it was cool to meet."

"You late, Slim—come on, hurry up." The lock buzzed, and I was in.

Success! I thought to myself, as I ran up the flight of stairs to his flat.

He opened the door in his usual white tee shirt, gold chain, and designer sweatpants. As I walked in, I was surprised by a crowd in his little apartment. They all looked at me in predatory silence. It was the first time I was nervous in the company of my San Francisco connection.

He asked how many I wanted this time and I was apprehensive to respond—at the risk of being robbed and beaten by the strangers. I wasn't here for a nickel bag of weed—there was a wad of cash on me for the buy.

My eyes fixed on Moog, to hide my fear from the rest of the room. "How many can you do?" He could sense I was nervous with the crowd and escorted me to the kitchen. "They cool, Slim. You good in my spot. They just acting hard—I got you."

Money and drugs exchanged hands. We spoke about a deal by mail, at the midway point of my trip—St. Louis. It was just one of the many chemical induced conversations people have on drugs. I never intended on mailing him any cash and he didn't think I was dumb enough to do so. In these situations, it's just our way of being cordial. The small talk of two people with only one thing in common.

As it was our final meeting, we did the thing where you shake hands and bro hug. I took a hit of the dose he prepared during our exchange of pleasantries and I never saw him again.

THE NEXT MORNING, Betty and I checked out of the hotel. This would be the first time I didn't have to pay the $300 deep cleaning fee for smoking pot in my room on my many visits here. After the first time this happened, I decided not to smoke in the room anymore to avoid the charge. But the pot I had with me on my second visit stunk so bad I was charged anyway. That meant I had to smoke every time, on principal. It got to the point in the past few visits that I offered to pay the fee up front. I didn't give a shit, and they loved taking my money. Betty was a stickler for following rules and very frugal, so I had to refrain from my exercise of "principles." Next stop Vegas, and wedded bliss.

On our way to Vegas, we drove through Steinbeck Country—lush valleys surrounded by dreary brown mountains—I couldn't help but think of the migrant workers, Woody Guthrie, the old black and white photos of post-depression America, and The Lonesome LA Cowboy "hanging out and hanging on."

Thinking that if I had money in my pocket and we got married, the man I had become would be forced out and forgotten. But addiction is a wound that cuts deep. In time it can be healed, but the scars always remain.

Through Bakersfield and into Nevada, we were both looking forward to the unknown madness of Las Vegas. It's the first time I gave thought to the 308 gram gorilla I had stashed in the back. Very few states on our way home would be as understanding of such a parcel as California.

I wouldn't share the knowledge of the package with Betty. It would ruin the trip with anxiety. Another reason was trying to protect myself from her nervous behavior, in the event we were pulled over. We found Vegas as the low autumn sun swept toward California. Excited for the future and very much in love, we checked into the honeymoon suite.

I got the room key and sent Betty and the bags to the room with the porter. I drove the Toyota to the parking garage and got high. There was always a scheme running about how I could get a little distance from the one whom I had spent so much time away from—just to satisfy my lust for another hit.

She knew I had a small stash of pot for the road trip, but had no idea about my meetings with Moog. As far as she knew, I was off the shit. That was the unspoken reason I left Philly for California in the first place—to get off the shit. The spoken reason was to make a ton of cash.

Getting high was not as difficult to hide on the road as one would think. Something was always in my pocket that I could toss down the gullet while she was distracted with sightseeing. It was actually more difficult to hide in the hotel, as I preferred to ingest these drugs nasally. I had to figure out a way to prepare a dose ahead of time that could be snorted quickly.

It took approximately two to three minutes to prepare the drugs for ingestion, but only three seconds to snort. This was the problem. I could only use the bathroom excuse once or twice a day before it was obvious. How would I get away with it?

When I got to the room, the answer was sitting on the coffee table: a box of wooden matches placed by the maid. The box was emptied of its matches and I prepared my next hit inside. Then I returned the box with prepared dose on the coffee table, in plain sight. I had a technique of rolling a dollar bill with one hand inside my pocket. As Betty went to the kitchen, or bathroom, or to answer the phone, I would pull the rolled bill out and I'm fixed. Her blind trust for the man she loved would be betrayed again and again.

We did some gambling, and I won. I won a lot. Looking back, it was like our relationship to this point—I took wild risks and my luck held-fast. Betty took measured risks and lost every time. She was always the one who paid the price for my irresponsible behaviors. Meanwhile, I walked away satisfied and relatively unscathed.

We walked around the strip and neither of us were very amused at the tawdry nature of it all. Everything had a thin facade in this town. Behind all of the flashing lights and fancy restaurants, there was no real substance to be found. Nothing that spoke to any deep part of the soul. If you weren't here to lose your money or your mind, it was a waste of time.

The Matchbox (photo by Rob Kaniuk)

We came to Vegas for two reasons—witness the madness and get married. Disenchanted with the spectacle, we took the winnings from my long night of drugs and baccarat to buy a ring and get ourselves a marriage certificate from the courthouse. All of the pertinents in hand, we found the most ridiculous name we could in the yellow pages—The Hollywood Wedding Chapel. Choices for officiating this sacred moment in our lives included Elvis and Marilyn Monroe. We chose for a "traditional service" and had to rent a witness named Manuel (who doubled as our limo driver).

THE MORNING SUN brought us to wake as a married couple, at the beginning of our new life together. I ordered room service—fresh squeezed orange juice, an arrangement of fruit, and scrambled eggs. After breakfast we made our way to the cage to cash in the rest of my winnings, then checked out of the hotel and Las Vegas.

The Grand Canyon would be the first stop of many on the honeymoon. There was a loose itinerary that included: the Grand Canyon, southeast to Austin, TX, northeast to Memphis, due north to St. Louis, then east to Central Illinois for Thanksgiving with Betty's parents.

November in the southwest is windy but warm in the afternoon—warm enough to have worn shorts as we left the strip. It took only an hour to get to The Hoover Dam, and we stopped to take pictures and walk across the time zone. The area was suffering from a drought and Lake Mead had a ring of calcium all around the edges, marking the pre-drought waterline. It made me sad to see this measured retreat. There was no denying the situation when the bright white ring stood shining in your face.

It must be human nature to look away and protect ourselves. If only Betty could have seen it, and insulated herself from what I had become. Deep in the core, hidden from the world—I had become hollow. Anything tied to me would collapse under the weight of lies and deception. Logic noticed a problem, but love denied it. Soon, it would be too late.

In Kingman, AZ we stopped for gas and a bite to eat. I smoked a bowl and snorted a dose prepared before we left Vegas. It was about a forty five minute drive to the canyon, and we began to talk of what we'd do. Should we take a burro ride to the bottom? Helicopter tour? Do we dare hike the trail? It was exciting to think of the trip ahead. Along the road I noticed a vehicle, way off in the sagebrush.

"Did you see that?"

"See what?" Betty said, oblivious.

"A cop car, or Border Patrol. It was way off in the bushes back there. Kinda shady looking."

This caused me to snap out of the warm nod I had going since Kingman. Scanning my rearview, I saw a wall of dust leading from the sagebrush to the road. "Well, looks like we are getting pulled over."

"What are you talking about? I don't see any cops."

He was about a minute behind us as he pulled onto the highway, but we were the only car from here to the horizon—I was sure he was after us.

It turned into a standoff at seventy-five miles an hour. He studied my truck with the tarpaulin carefully fastened to the bed, Pennsylvania tags glaring back at him. I kept darting my eyes from rear-view to road and back again, never moving the position of my head.

Noticeably peering into the rear-view mirror is the look of guilt to any officer, but the passenger turning around to look might as well be a signed confession. With this in mind, I told Betty to follow my lead. "Keep your head forward and do not worry."

After ten agonizing minutes, the officer changed lanes and began to pass me. A wave of relief came over the two of us when I saw the move to overtake and said to Betty, "We're good, he's going to pass us finally."

It felt like he was behind us for hours. The neat little package, wrapped in vacuum sealed bags was moved from the grenade box mounted to the frame of the truck and planted firmly in the front of my mind.

As he passed I turned to Betty like we were in a conversation, oblivious to who was behind us this whole time. The police SUV got to where he could get a look at me and he rapidly decelerated, dropped behind me once again, and hit the lights.

It's okay I thought, *I've been through this plenty of times before.* Betty was nervous about the little bowl I smoked in Kingman. I was thinking more about the package in the box, the drugs I bought in San Fran, and how utterly destroyed she would be.

I pulled over to the side and the officer approached the passenger side window. Betty was startled as he knocked on the window for her to roll it down, not a good start. License, registration, and proof of insurance was asked for—and provided. He asked if I knew why I was being stopped. I had no clue.

"Suspicion of driving while intoxicated. I was behind you and noticed that your tire hit the white line on the shoulder three times. Do you have anything in the vehicle I should know about? The reason I ask is that I smell a faint odor of marijuana coming from the truck."

I thought to myself, *Yea—$13,000 cash, three quarters of a pound of hash, thirty 80mg oxycontins (give or take a few), a half ounce of marijuana, and a meticulously dismantled 250-3000 Savage Arms rifle—with scope (that may or may not have a past all its own).*

"No officer, I do not."

He asked where we were coming from, and heading. I explained that I had lived in California for the past two years with work, we just got married less than twenty-four hours ago, and were heading back home to Philly.

"I'm just going to run your information and get you out of here." He went to run my information while we sat and waited.

What happened next flattened my tires to the rim—the officer exited the vehicle and instead of heading to hand me my paperwork, he walked to the back of his SUV and let his dog out.

My peripherals went dark, I could feel my heart pounding, I had to find a way to save Betty before the whole weight of the situation took her down as well.

I CAN'T REMEMBER the name of either officer, but I'll never forget the name of that damn barking dog—Eliot Ness. I shit you not. Eliot fucking Ness. This dog was going ape-shit—about to have a coronary as he feverishly alerted on every last piece of inventory in the blue Toyota. The four-legged bastard was losing it—barking, scratching the truck, chasing his tail, completely confused of which way to turn. All I could think was, *great—now this fucking dog is gonna keel over and I'll be charged with the death of a law officer.*

"My dog has alerted on multiple sections of the truck. With this being a heavy drug-trafficking corridor, I'll be searching the truck and its contents."

Oh, you don't say? I thought.

Backup arrived and the truck was being torn apart. Every detail of my past two years in California was being meticulously inventoried by two officers and a K9. Golf clubs, work tools, winter clothes, summer clothes, souvenirs from the places I've been, books, CDs, DVDs. When you live on a pot farm for two years—handling, processing, harvesting, and of course smoking pot—everything gets corrupted with the skunk-like scent of marijuana.

With the threat of a crowbar to dismantle the truck and Betty's freedom at stake, I relented and gave up the package. Eliot went back to the SUV to have a victory bark and the two officers retrieved the Vietnam-era grenade box, fixed to the chassis. In it, they found the brick.

Cuffed and sitting on the side of the road, Betty was removed for questioning. She told the truth—she knew nothing of any package, or the origins of the package. The attention came to me and I assured them she had absolutely no knowledge of any drugs. I was asked if I wanted to cooperate and I agreed.

"Where did this come from?"

"I made it."

"If you aren't going to cooperate, you leave me no choice but to take you and your wife to jail."

The "california" stamp was a thing that I found amusing upon inception, but the officers now thought I was part of some California marijuana cartel. I couldn't help but laugh at the ridiculous claim—my dismissive laughter was not well-received by the boys in blue.

"I'm the guy you're looking for. She has nothing to do with this. You caught the guy who made the drugs, there's nobody to give up—you got him. I'm the head of your "California cartel."

I was placed in the backseat of the SUV, where Eliot had been barking himself silly for the past hour. This was part of my punishment for being "uncooperative." Now that the target of his assault was in the same car, the barking grew louder and without pause. 3/16 inch plexiglass with round air holes on six inch centers is not a comfortable barrier between man and beast. I never wanted to fight a dog before or since, but I would've choked the eyes out of Eliot Ness if it meant just one minute of silence.

MY RIGHT EAR was about to bleed as Mr. Ness continued his incessant barking when I saw everything I listed in my head, laid out on the tailgate of my truck—the cash, the drugs, and the gun. The officer approached and I hoped it was to tell Eliot to shut the fuck up, or to open a window and let the clamor dissipate into the night air.

"You're lucky you know how to break down a gun and store it properly, or you'd be charged with a firearm too. Do you have any more cash in the vehicle?"

"No sir, that'd be all of it."

"Okay, the amount of drugs together with that much cash—we are going to take possession of the vehicle and property in it."

With that, a call was made to the impound lot to dispatch a tow truck. We had been on the side of the road long enough that the warm sun had set and the southwesterly winds picked up to a sustained gale —I was freezing cold in my shorts and tee. Six hours searching my truck was enough for these officers, so when the dispatcher for the tow company informed them it would be a two hour wait, they were not happy.

"You just got a big break. I'm not waiting two hours for a tow truck, so I have decided to release the truck and property to your wife."

I didn't imagine when we got married an overweight, self-satisfied, arresting officer would be the first person to describe Betty as my wife. I was relieved that she wasn't going to jail, but she would have to now learn the temperament of the blue Toyota's manual gearbox—in Arizona—all by herself—on our honeymoon.

Eliot was still barking at me from top to bottom when I observed a thirty second tutorial administered to Betty on how to drive stick-shift. She asked if it was possible to follow the officer to jail in Prescott. He said, "You can try." With that, Mr. Personality came back and got into the driver seat and took off like a flash—leaving Betty perfectly lost.

We made it to jail in the wild west town of Prescott, Arizona in time for lights out. An old timey jail with bars and about 10 men in each of the four cells that surrounded a common area filled with stainless steel dining benches. I had been in jail before, but this was totally different. It felt like I was in the movies; all I needed was a tin cup to drag along the bars in lament.

I was able to call Betty the next day, and she was crying the whole time. I asked her to leave me there but she wouldn't. She was willing to stay as long as it would take to get me out. I called the next day and she was still crying. Betty wouldn't leave. I explained to her that I admired her fierce loyalty, but she would have to get back to Philly to begin working on my release.

When I left California, I took a partial payment of cash and the rest of my earnings were sent with Hamburger Hank back to Philly in the form of product. I needed to get word to my man back east to liquidate the product as soon as possible.

Betty made some calls from the busted down motel located across the street from the courthouse. One call was to her father—explaining her honeymoon and the urgent need for a lawyer; another was made to Jack—my guy in Philly who had the product.

BY THE THIRD NIGHT it was time to move a group of us from the quaint comfort of the courthouse basement to the Yavapai County Detention Center. YCDC felt more appropriate for the full weight of my situation. The charge for hash is a bit more severe than a simple marijuana conviction—it's considered a "manufactured/dangerous drug" and carries the same penalties as heroin in Arizona—the same penalties as having three quarters of a pound of crack-cocaine. I was in deep shit. This is where people in deep shit end up; and there was nothing misdemeanor or quaint about this setting.

Once I made it into a cell block and my bunk, the worst withdrawal I would ever endure was peaking. It's one thing to perform the daily constitutional with company in your cell; it is quite another to be pissing out your ass with little or no warning. Take the toilet issues—add night sweats, body aches, and constant migraines—my time there was less than copacetic.

Withdrawal symptoms and the obsession to get high had part of my mind consumed at all times. Another part was constantly running over schemes and plans to raise the 25K it would take to post bond. But there was a part of my mind—my conscience—that I was trying my best to suppress.

Betty and the disappointment I had caused, the pain in her trembling voice over the jailhouse phone, her commitment to stand by her man no matter what—those thoughts crept in and destroyed me each time. I had to keep focused and not appear weak in my present company.

Observation is the best tool to have when trying to toe the line in jailhouse hierarchy. It is mostly all posturing and bravado, but the most dangerous guys are quiet and prickly. I took the first three days to get off the toilet and keep quiet while I kept an eye out for who was given the most respect in the common area.

Who picks what we watch on TV? Who gets donations of hard boiled eggs every morning, before so much as a fork touches a tray? Who are the guys at each table the others look to for a smile of approval when a joke is made? These are the guys who run their respective crews. Where does each crew sit? Which crew is friendly with the other? These are all answers that you would find out, but it was important that I found out on my own—without any "help."

Don't ever ask for favors, but definitely do ask about house rules (shower schedules, race relations, chores and the such). Again, not something you want to find out after the fact. If you have to fight, punch first— as hard as you can—right in the fucking throat (thanks Jeremy). Keeping my head down for the first week and not speaking to anyone unless I was invited to a conversation, I didn't have to punch any throats. Thank god for that. My stature would not be able to sustain very much physical battle—my home field was of the mind.

I noticed that the clear leader of this cell block was an older white man from my home state. We were the only guys there from PA, and he wasn't going to let anything bad happen to me—unless I deserved it. That, and the fact that I had such a high secured bond, earned a certain amount of respect.

As for the bond I had to post; a secured bond must be met in full. This means no bail bondsmen, no ten percent—it would take either $25,000 cash or equivalent collateral. I didn't have a house to put up, but I had a few good friends who tried to offer theirs. But we were in the midst of the mortgage crisis, so it wouldn't work out—everyone had already refinanced. I had to come up with the cash.

JACK WAS A FRIEND that I grew up with and trusted very much. One problem I had was that Jack had a seasonal business he was funding with the profits of my package from 'ol Hamburger. The money was tied up until the season was over and neither of us expected to need it so soon. It was time to make the call. The call was to an "employer."

I had a lot of information that could be used to completely drop all charges against me—and my employer knew it. I directed Betty to call my sister and relay the message that I needed to borrow the 25K until I got out. The call was made. The money was delivered.

Murph would act as courier, and go my bail. Murph is a frail, nervous, out-of-his-element alcoholic, that loves his son. He got a one-way ticket to Phoenix, where he would meet Betty's step-brother, Chaz, who was living there at the time.

This big bastard stood six foot four—two hundred sixty lbs. He picked Betty up weeks earlier and drove the blue Toyota the ninety miles to Phoenix with his knees up around his chin. Chaz lived in a foreclosed home he bought when the bubble popped, with the plan to flip it. The garage would be the perfect location to park the Toyota.

Murph landed, knuckles and elbows sore from clutching the blue duffel bag like it was the crown jewels of Poland for the past six hours. Chaz was about an hour late to pick up Murph and when they arrived at his hovel, Murph slept on the floor for a wink or two before he made the trip to Yavapai County Correctional Facility, in Camp Verde.

It was a day before that I was sitting on my bunk, watching the sunrise over the mountains when I realized there was something missing on my long list of charges. Come to think of it I don't remember seeing it on the tailgate with the rest of my nefarious inventory—the oxy's. I leapt from the bunk and rifled through all of my paperwork to see if I could find any mention of my precious rations. There was nothing. However, I did notice that the rough sum of $13,000 cash that was seized was writ-

172 / Schuylkill Valley Journal

ten up as $5,820—those fuckers got must have split the rest. Oh well, what's gone is gone, no matter what the number on the paper says—I would never get a dollar of that money back.

I had put the score from Moog in an Advil PM bottle because of the similarity in shape, size, and color. The officers must have seen them. They searched that truck for six hours—I know they found them. Was it a charge that would appear later? Yet another felony to the list? Or maybe, just maybe this was gonna be a high time with me in a deep nod, and Murph driving eastbound.

Only someone in my shoes would understand. Getting high didn't get me here, it wasn't my fault—being pulled over by a cop who didn't have a good reason to stop me got me here. Just bad luck. Just universal luck breaking even for my taking Vegas for over seven thousand big ones. It could be justified in any number of ways. But it was never the fault of my number one fan, my confidant, my mistress—my drug. All I could think about since I found out Murph was on his way was finding that bottle and dipping slowly, back into the void.

Murph got in that truck and it started right up. He couldn't believe how solid that damn Toyota was. I got up that morning and paced around the day room like a lone goldfish kissing the edge of the bowl in never ending circles. I was anxious to be on my way as soon as possible—not sure how long I would be a free man, I wanted to take full advantage of my time before the trial and the prospect of nine years behind bars.

Murph arrived right when he said he would, 8:30 A.M. What he didn't know was that the clerks at the correctional facility were not used to people coming in with a duffel bag—filled with cash. When he began to slip each of the twenty five separate thousand dollar bundles through the slot in the window, they asked him, "Why didn't you just bring a check?"

And what the clerks didn't know was that drug dealers didn't usually write checks.

After miscounting the cash four different times, they had to call the boss into the room to count it herself. It was all there, just as Murph had pleaded several times.

I was growing nervous in the cell block and the guys were starting to tease me a bit.

"Nobody's coming for you."

"I knew you didn't have no twenty five stacks, you're full of shit."

The door buzzed, a guard opened it and said, "Con-e-uck?"

"That's me!"

"Roll your shit up, you made bail."

I was never so happy to hear some asshole mispronounce my last name. I packed up my shit and gave one last look around—as to say, "told you so, fuckers."

The shorts I had on when I left the strip were waiting for me in processing. It had snowed the night before, but I didn't care one bit. I walked out of that place with shorts and a t-shirt, hugged Murph, and got on the road.

I called to thank my lawyer on our way out of Arizona and he said, "Whatever you do, do not tell me where you are right now. As a condition of your bail agreement, you still don't have permission to leave the state. I'll contact you when the judge signs the papers allowing you to leave. In the meantime, drive safely."

We stopped for a bite to eat and some gas. I looked in the 50 cal. ammo-box that was my center console and found the bottle with every last oxy 80 still in there. It was on. I took a deep breath and disappointed everyone who fought so hard to get me home as I inhaled a huge dose while Murph was in the bathroom of the restaurant.

I would love to tell you that I learned a lesson in Yavapai County, that I wanted to change, that I was a good husband from that day forward. However, nothing but pure misery would lie beyond the horizon.

The lawyer called me back as I was kissing oblivion, three hours into New Mexico—it was safe to leave.

I was gone.

A POETRY WORKSHOP AT GRATERFORD PRISON

by Fran B.

In January, 2017, I started a poetry workshop at Graterford Prison. I had wanted to do this for a long time, several years, and my semi-retirement enabled me to think that I finally had the time to devote to the project. Early in my career as a psychotherapist I had worked in the Philadelphia Jail System and had, over the years, developed a specialty in addictions and criminal justice; teaching college-level courses in criminal behavior, treating offenders with substance abuse issues, and writing my doctoral dissertation about the developmental life course of men who had been both incarcerated and addicted and who had exited successfully from both and established productive lives. As a poet with these professional experiences, I fully expected to find poets at Graterford Prison.

Through mutual friends, I was put in touch with some folks from the Prison Literacy Project who arranged for me to meet with a group of inmates representing an organization in Graterford Prison called Lifers, Inc. We had two initial planning meetings in October and November of 2016. The members of the group were curious about why I wanted to limit the group to 7–8 participants and "lifers" or long-term inmates. I explained that I wanted to keep the group small (eight at most) so that each participant would have a chance to share his poetry each week and to long-termers so there would be consistency in attendance and each would have a chance to really develop their poetic skills over time. I wanted the workshop to be open-ended and continuous. They were excited by the proposal and agreed to advertise the workshop and seek entries (two poems per person) for consideration. They collected poems from approximately 12 individuals and I reviewed the entries and picked eight participants out of 11 entries. The process took several months. The entries ranged from "raw talent" to already published poets. Of the initial eight, one never showed, two dropped out after the first meeting, and I met with the remaining five once a week since January, 2017. Since then, two of the five original have been attending sporadically and two additional members (who initially applied but didn't make the first "cut") have been added since September, 2017.

I was interested in passing on my experience as a poet over the 53 years I have been writing and the 33 years (off and on with interruptions) that I have been coming out of the isolation of my writing and seeking and benefitting from feedback from other poets through workshops and the support and feedback from the community of poets in the Greater Philadelphia region and nationally, through my participation in the Antioch Writers' Workshop (AWW) in Yellow Springs, Ohio. Workshops have not only widened my exposure to modern, contemporary poets, it has "toughened my skin" so that feedback has become a means of improving and developing my voice and not just an unpleasant assault on my sensitivity to be endured. Without developing this openness to others' reactions and observations of my work, I recognize that my poetic voice would not have developed and grown stronger, more precise, and more mature. I was hoping to bring this same experience of developing the art of voice to the men at Graterford.

By design, I wanted to conduct the workshop like the ones I have experienced at AWW in Yellow Springs, Ohio where I studied with Cathy Smith Bowers, John Drury and Jamey Dunham and, locally, my experience in Grant Clauser's *Wordshop* supported by the Montgomery County Poet Laureate Program. The most powerful workshop experience, however, has been with Leonard Gontarek as a member of the Osage Poets.

Borrowing from all of these experiences, I began by introducing some guidelines about feedback to the participants: find something you like or that strikes you, makes you react emotionally, to the poem, and give feedback to the poet that tries to focus on "specifics," why you liked something or didn't like it, what about the work (its rhythm, content, turn of phrase, its metaphors or images) make you think it is effective or not; and how the poem could be improved. I usually lead off the feedback and the others follow. The discussions about the poems, and poetry in general, as well as life, writing, prison, the world at large, have been wide-ranging, sometimes passionate, and always illuminating. The poets have been open to the feedback and have the opportunity to take the feedback and suggested edits and redo the poem.

The caliber of the poetry has consisted of a range of quality from the work of first-time writers that reveal a raw talent and sensibility, to that of more experienced writers that show development and past experience but that also suggest room for growth to more clearly express core emotion and less intellectual "preachiness." That said, I am stunned by the caliber of the work, the hunger to improve, the openness to the feedback, not only from myself but each other, and the desire to take themselves and their development as a poet seriously.

Examples of some of the prompts include:

Self Portrait Prompt: Who are you? We all have multiple identities; man, worker, old, young, who you use to be, who you are now, where you came from, where you live now, a skill or talent that you possess, memories that you have, possibly regrets. Write a poem about yourself, who you are or who you would like to be. As you can see from the handouts, different poets have handled this in different ways. Some choose to describe themselves by describing who they are in a relationship, a son to a father, a husband/boyfriend to a wife/girlfriend. Some choose to focus on a day, making a catalogue of going through a day, what they like musically or to eat, where the day might take them, describing their surroundings, their environment.

As in this example, I hand out poems written by others (or myself) that illustrate a response in some way to the prompt.

Another example: Here are two very different poems about BIG subjects, one about war ("Plato told" by e.e. cummings), the other about death ("Spring and Fall: To a young child" by Gerard Manley Hopkins). They are "alike" in that they are "trying to impart wisdom or give advice"— the first about war to a dead/wounded soldier (or to us as readers who survived); the second, to a child (and really, to us as readers). Write a poem about death or war giving advice or imparting wisdom to someone (could be yourself).

I have included in the prompts a wide range of subjects and styles, from haiku to sonnet, and prompts that have forced an economy of thought and expression.

Example: Write a poem that gets shorter with each line. Start your poem with a piece of advice.

As a guide to respond to this prompt, I used one of my own, unpublished poems.

American Eclipse

Don't look at the sun.
Shadows deceive.
The moon hides
In daylight,
Pulls us
To its
Fire.

The poems these men have written in response have been remarkable. Sometimes raw and in need of editing, at times insightful, wise and vivid; and the poets are learning to re-write and re-visit their work, developing that most important question that I have found to propel my own work forward: How can I improve this poem?

It continues to be a powerful experience to facilitate this workshop and to learn from and share with these men. I hope you enjoy their work.

A NOTE ON THE SELECTIONS

Although all of the poems that were submitted have merit, this particular group of five poets display special talent and affinity for poetry. Poetic talent can appear anywhere, under any circumstances, because it is the result of the inner human drive to evolve and connect. These five poets transcend situational concerns and rise to a universal level that communicates to our shared humanity. Their poems have in common an emotional intensity but each poet sings with his own unique voice.

Reggie L. evokes inner dreamscapes with rich images and strong rhythms in *An Army of Angels* and *Gauguin's Dream*. Terrell C. uses short, breath-based lines to give expression to his deep feelings of regret in *The Ghost*. In Portrait, he questions who he is instead of writing the typical self-portrait that does the opposite. Ben C. in *The Future of My Father's Past*, explores his identity too, and the moral connection between father and son. *Aretha* by Aaron F., is a tapestry of city street images that describe and evoke the feeling of soul music in long, luxurious lines. His poem *The Wanderers* uses the short breath-lines of rap to describe his far flung family. Finally, Eduardo R. presents us with three poems that are the work of a gifted natural poet whose work would be publishable in any literary magazine. Note the diversity of his approach and his precise, musical language in *Jabaro's Song, [Un]fixed Positions* and *Apology*.

Taken together, these poems are a testimony to the fact that the mind can be free though the body is not. These poets bring a new meaning to "outside the box." I am grateful that they can.

—Eric Greinke

AN ARMY OF ANGELS

Reginald L.

I do, indeed, remember them,
dancing in the slatted shadows of my death row cell,
diaphanous, floating across the ceiling, strafing the walls,
falling, falling, like dust motes.

I do recall them whispering
down the cold, hollowed cell block where I heard
their maddening screams in the wind, rising and falling
on snow truffles, their deep baritones sliding
through the steel grate of my mind.

And I am certain I saw one
or two of them in the grainy depths of old photographs,
in the multiple identities and split personalities of the ink-splotched
splatter in letters, in the intricate discernible patterns
of unbreakable habits.

Years later, transported into another strange
world, into a higher consciousness, where detection of indistinguishable
features skulk behind crisp, sharp-pressed uniforms or white lab coats,
or

the unheralded intrusion of volunteers, thespians and trolls
wedded in a symbiosis of wicked or benign plots,
large hawk eyes squinting and flitting back and forth
past the gray-blanched clouds swirling above the mindless chatter
of brain-addled zombies, strange creatures morphed into silence.

Up, up, up over the walls of a gifted tribe,
ghosts in the secrets of the arts, the language of the invisible, the unseen
where mine is an army of angels.

GAUGUIN'S DREAM

Reginald L.

And did I ever tell you about the finer qualities that you possess,
A delicate sweetness that drips like honey into the valley of my soul?
How the very thought of you conjures bright moonbeams that illumine
The darkness of my cell, how the brightest stars form your lovely face?
Would you mind if I stare too long, ogle the diamonds of your eyes,
The brilliance of your smile, the plush cherry lips, the perfect symmetry
Of your burnished brown cheeks? The golden light of a tropical sun
Leaps from your long silken black tresses as I wander aimlessly, slowly,
Through this exotic forest, on the island of Gauguin's dream.

THE GHOST

Terrell C.

They took us from her
chained and shackled
long before I was born.
She tried to get us back
blood made our skin slick
and we slipped through her grasp.
Thunder sticks and cat-o-nines
were the tools to keep her at bay.
All she could do was watch
as we passed the point of no return.

She loved us, though,
and her cries became
the rhythm that ran through our blood,
gave us strength,
as we rode the rough seas of sorrow,
fighting the nauseating sway
of floating coffins,
while our tears ran free,
mixing with the excrement
of captivity.

We arrived,
standing naked, bloodied
and broken on blocks made of wood.
We cried, we cried,
Oh God, why have you
forsaken us so?
Our pleas echoed through
the vast emptiness of space and time,
unheard, unanswered.
Tears sparkled off
black skin like liquid diamonds,
as we faced the heavens
yearning for those gentle kisses of the sun

that now burned our bodies with shame.
It was all in vain,
as if the heavens themselves
had turned against us.

Through it all
We tried to
hold on to the memory of her
to keep us sane
while lost and enslaved
in a strange, insane
and hostile place.

Then we died, we died …

and to the next of us
she was only a ghost,
haunting the fringes of awareness.
They told us
she was backward, uncivilized,
and we believed them.
Collective amnesia
spread like the flu,
we were forced to mis-remember
who she was,
who we were.
We lost our names,
our religion,
our language, our God,
and many, by the way we act,
we even lost our minds.
We became
remade in the image
of those who stole us.

She still haunts us though
you can feel her anger,
in the beat of our music,
see her presence

in the rhythm of our dance.
And when we lift our voices,
you can hear traces of her sorrow
in the songs we sing.

PORTRAIT

Terrell C.

I have lived thousands of lives
Each one leaving a little bit behind
As hard to reach as a soul.

Lost
In possibilities,
Who am I?

      Is
The gap in my teeth,
The darkness of my skin,
The bow in my legs,
The brown in my eyes,
The curl of my hair,
      Me?
Passed down through generations,
Like heirlooms,
A walking, talking
Duplication of those who came before?

Or is the portrait
Of who I am
Every bit that I inherited,
A mosaic of biology,
Each piece a main ingredient
To the uniqueness
Of who I am?

THE FUTURE OF MY FATHER'S PAST

Ben C.

As a boy I searched non-stop
to find my reflection in a mirror,
find my father in the surface
of the glass that reflected the soul
of a half-breed black sheep.

Was I the product of a slow breath
into the womb of a troubled woman
thought worthy or the abstract of
two conscious thoughts induced by
liquor, drugs and music? I am only

what I am. Ouija boards and terror
cards couldn't bring the remedy I
sought, a child stuck alone in gray.
No leading figures nor alphas were
Worthy. I called out to my sister's
King to hear my voice, embrace it,

Dad. It didn't feel right and I was
ashamed. I was angry, never to feel
the passion of Luther's wish to dance
with my father again. Again, as if
it had ever happened once upon ...

Coming of age was strange when
I looked into her cradle and promises
were made to never fade like vapor.
Her smile was a drug, an inspiration.

In the eleventh cycle, under the fallen
leaf moon, past met future, the present
was born. I faded to black, became
to her what haunted my childhood,
a broken promise, left snow white
with the crazy queen who embraced

the willie lynch project, father against
daughter, girl hates her first love.

I wake in a cell, handcuffs rubbing
against my veins, the ghost of my
father's past had become my future.

ARETHA

Aaron F.

Summertime in the city
Saturday morning, a little before noon
The strip is bustling, shoppers and pick pockets,
Hawkers and vendors, boosters and con men,
Each plying their trade, the beat cop picking up envelopes.

Young girls sit on stoops braiding each other's hair,
Barely finish, breaking off the steps into a round of double dutch.
A game of Deadman in the street, Muchie and JoJo playing step ball
On Ms. Lucille's front steps, Ron Ron and his crew
a game of stickball in the church lot.

Meanwhile, little Mackie Brown is getting his hustle on
Outside the Count Down Lounge, sitting on his shoeshine box
Popping his rag on his customer's black knob-toed Stacy Adams.
The front door is open, the jukebox is blasting, you would think
A live show was going on. "You're a no good heartbreaker,
         a liar and a cheat,
I don't know why you treat me the way you do."

It's that slow, mournful moan of Aretha, pouring her heart out,
In a story of unappreciated love, attacking the atmosphere,
Rolling like lava, overpowering everyone within sound and reach.

Aretha was a teenage mother married early to the father of
         her two sons.
He was much older and seasoned, a player out of Detroit, unfaithful and
Abusive. "My friends keep telling me, you ain't no good,
         they don't know why
I stay around, I'd leave you if I could."

Babs is behind the bar, a stunning beauty from Trinidad,
Pouring whiskey and holding court to numbers writers, other
Hustlers, male and female, waiting for that lead number to come out.
Cigarette and cigar smoke hover at the ceiling, perfume and cologne

Mingle indiscriminately. The smell of Ida Mae's fried chicken
Invades the room from the kitchen as she prepares for the noon crowd.

They'll eat, drink, converse and settle down, waiting for the number,
While Aretha bangs on the piano keys like she's banging on the door
Of her cheating lover, lamenting her heartache. "I ain't never
      loved a man
The way I love you."

THE WANDERERS

Aaron F.

Aunt Sadie was the first
To take the wandering
The oldest, fourteen
When she left

She wanted to go
To school, hesitated in
New York, a brief stop,
Then dropped in
Waterbury, Connecticut

Next to go
Uncle Talley, nine
He claims he walked
To New York

I asked why,
He said he was tired
Walking behind a plow
Everyday, up one row
Down another, he was
Walking to New York
Anyway

Aunt Rosie, man,
She a beauty, tall
Copper tone, long hair
Big almond eyes that
Speak to the soul

Went to Detroit
The Motor City
Dreams not met, no
Regrets, save your
Pity for the needy

Aunt Lillibell and
Uncle Woodrow
Went to Baltimore
She's the prankster
Of the crew

Woodrow, a kind and
Gentle soul
He raised his daughter,
Rosalie's too

My mom was
The last to flee
The nest, she
Came to Philly
With my dad and
Three of my siblings

I was the first
Born in this new land
We call home

Scattered like seeds
In the wind, taking root,
Never to return

JIBARO'S SONG

Eduardo R.

At the root of the coffee tree
is a germ of blood
spilled by the migrant farmer.
The scent of earth
grooved under his fingernails
is the account of his body's worth.
Burnt onto his back
by the torch of the sun
are the lyrics to a field song—

> Above the green heights
> Of my borinquen nation
> Maricao rises
> Amidst the plantation

For a piece of land
where arthritic hands
will wring an ounce of coffee
for every gallon of sweat,
a man will work his whole life;
a family will huddle
under a corrugated tin roof;
a congregation will meet
under the watchful eyes
of a mysterious God;
the hills will sing of Maricao:

> where an ancient sigh
> blows in the breeze
> to caress the mountain
> and bless the trees.

[UN]FIXED POSITIONS

Eduardo R.

in the meta-analysis
of an object observing itself,
objectivity is the wished-for goal
through the parallax view
of a subjective lens.

a man can be too close to himself
to name himself;
the crowd may be too far away
to know him intimately.

the hypotenuse of a triangle
is the squared sum
of the length on one side squared
plus the length of the other side squared:
$a^2 + b^2 = c^2$.

i am one leg running away
on an x-axis;
the reason between myself and why
grows in the shadows of tall trees.

the distance from a star
is measured by the fixed position
between that star and the sun
triangulated with a baseline
equal to the radius of the earth.

translation: you and i,
equidistant, vying for the same light,
the same air,
a straight line between us
rising, like a wall—
and we keep looking up
at a vast expanse of sky
that we wish we could touch.

objects in a mirror
appear closer than they are.

with ever-changing lengths
come ever-changing distances:
the flame cannot tell you its temperature;
the wind cannot gauge its own speed;
air is unaware of its visibility.
all objects are defined
in relation to other objects:
the melted candle,
a swirling leaf,
a pilot –
in flight or grounded.

all relations are subject to change
depending upon conditions:
a happy marriage,
a broken home,
an erect building,
a parking lot.

but there,
in the liminal spaces
between consciousness
and rapid eye movement,
where the science of seeing
cannot be certain
of anything at all,
there an objective truth is revealed:

a method exists in which
unfixed positions,
warped planes,
winding curves,
can be hammered into a perspective
(or an approximation thereof)
where an object can be known
(with at least theoretical precision)
and an explanation can be held
with the religious fervor
of an unbending faith.

APOLOGY

Eduardo R.

She says   she still
loves me,   the scent
of my undershirt   still   wraps   around   her
on lonely nights when the empty   space beside her
fills the room with an uneasiness, like a broken toe.

She says
the stark quiet of our home is pierced,
sometimes,
by sounds she cannot unhear,
a song, a laugh, the hiss of air from compressed cushions
when she rises to leave a room.

I wait to hear
what she has yet to say, impatient
as a statue waiting to be dusted, wait until
the little lies that have cast long shadows into today
come into the light, deep wounds stitched shut.

Confrontation is not always facing a blinding sun,
resolution not always the closure that's needed.
An apology is not in the words one can say
but the words one can hear.
If you wait long enough,
you will hear what you want.

David Adès is the author of the chapbook *Only the Questions Are Eternal* and the books *Mapping the World* and *Afloat in Light*. He is an award winning Australian poet living in Sydney.

Fran B. studied with poet David Ignatow from 1982-1984 at the 92nd Street Y in New York City. He was a recipient of the Judson Jerome Poetry Scholarship at the Antioch Writers' Workshop. He was nominated for a Pushcart Prize for his poem, Neshaminy, published in the *Schuylkill Valley Journal*. He is an Adjunct Professor in the Criminal Justice Department at West Chester University where he teaches a graduate course in Criminal Behavior and the Law. He conducts a poetry workshop with inmates at Graterford Prison under the auspices of the Prison Literacy Project of Pennsylvania.

Peter Barlow is the author of *Little Black Dots* (Chatter House Press, 2017). His work has appeared in *Rosebud, The MacGuffin, The Homestead Review, Red Rock Review, Underground Voices,* and *Per Contra.* He is an adjunct professor of English at University of Detroit-Mercy.

Sandra Becker was Bucks County 2014 Poet Laureate. Her Books: *Dread Islands,* Kelsay Books 2015, *Imperfect Matter,* WordTech 2013, *At the Well of Flowers,* VAC 2011, *Foreign Bodies,* Carolina Wren 2004. *What Now, What Next,* Kelsay Books, Spring 2018.

Dick Bentley has published fiction, poetry, and memoir in over 260 magazines and anthologies. His books include *Post-Freudian Dreaming* and *A General Theory of Desire.* Dick has served on the board of the Modern Poetry Association (now known as the Poetry Foundation). Before teaching writing at the University of Massachusetts, Dick was Planning Director for the Boston Housing Authority. He is a Yale graduate with an MFA from Vermont College.

Joseph A. Chelius works as an editorial director for a healthcare communications company in the Philadelphia suburbs. His poetry collection, *The Art of Acquiescence,* was published by WordTech Communications in 2014. His poems have appeared recently in *Poet Lore, The American Journal of Poetry, Rattle,* and *rkvry Quarterly Literary Journal.*

Joe Cilluffo's poems have previously appeared in the *Schuylkill Valley Journal* as well as *Philadelphia Poets*, *Apiary*, and *Philadelphia Stories*. He was the Featured Poet for the Fall 2014 Edition of the *SVJ*, which nominated his poem, "Light," for the Pushcart Prize. Joe's first book of poetry, *Always in the Wrong Season*, was recently published by Kelsay Books and is available on Amazon.com.

Grant Clauser is the author of four poetry books including *Reckless Constellations* (winner of the 2016 Cider Press Review Book Award) and *The Magician's Handbook* (PS Books, 2017). Poems have appeared in *The American Poetry Review*, *Painted Bride Quarterly*, *Tar River Poetry* and others. @uniambic

Mike Cohen hosts Poetry Aloud and Alive at Philadelphia's Big Blue Marble Book Store. His articles on sculpture regularly appear in the *Schuylkill Valley Journal*. His wry writing has appeared in the *Mad Poets Review*, *Apiary Magazine*, *Fox Chase Review*, and other journals. Mike's poetry can be found at www.mikecohensays.com and in his book BETWEEN THE I'S.

Cynthia Darling is currently working toward an M.F.A. with the Bluegrass Writers Studio at Eastern Kentucky University. She holds an M.A. in English Literature from Boston College and has taught high school English at independent schools for the past 20 years. Cynthia recently participated in the 2017 Disquiet International Literary Conference in Lisbon, Portugal.

Allen X. Davis's short fiction appears or is forthcoming in *Gravel*, *Flash Fiction Magazine*, *Microfiction Monday Magazine*, *Madcap Review*, *A Quiet Courage*, *Barking Sycamores*, and *Empty Sink Publishing*.

Salvatore Difalco's work has appeared in print and online. He lives in Toronto.

Juditha Dowd's work appears in *Poet Lore*, *Florida Review*, *Ekphrasis*, *Spillway*, *Kestrel* and elsewhere. She performs with the Cool Women ensemble locally and on the West Coast. *Poetry Daily* and *Verse Daily* have featured poems from her recent collection, "Mango in Winter."

W. D. Ehrhart teaches history and English at the Haverford School, where he also coaches Winter Track and sponsors the Poetry Club. His most recent publication is a 2017 chapbook from Adastra Press, *Praying at the Altar.*

Alfred Encarnacion's poems appeared in *Indiana Review, North American Review, The Paterson Literary Review.* He has work in *Blues Poems, The Open Boat, Unsettling America. The Outskirts of Karma* and *Ambassadors of the Silenced* are his two books.

R.G. Evans's books include *Overtipping the Ferryman, The Noise of Wings,* and *The Holy Both.* His original music was featured in the poetry documentaries *All That Lies Between Us* and *Unburying Malcolm Miller.* Evans teaches high school and college English and Creative Writing in southern New Jersey.

Linda M. Fischer has poems recently published or forthcoming in *Ibbetson Street, Iodine Poetry Journal, Muddy River Poetry Review, Poetry East, Potomac Review, Roanoke Review, Valparaiso Poetry Review, Verse-Virtual,* and *The Worcester Review.* www.lindamfischer.com

Ray Greenblatt's poetry has been published around the world, translated into Gaelic, Polish and Japanese, as well as set to music at the University of Siena in Italy. He has been on the Board of the Philadelphia Writers Conference and spoken at the John Steinbeck Festival in Salinas, California. His books include *Shadow with Green Eyes* (Meg Kennedy Press) and *Twenty Years on Graysheep Bay* (Sunstone Press).

Eric Greinke's poems have been published in hundreds of American and international journals and anthologies since the early 1970s. His most recent books are *Poets In Review* and *Zen Duende—Collaborative Poems* (with Glenna Luschei), both from Presa Press. He is currently finishing a book about poetic collaboration, to be called *In The 3rd Person.* www.ericgreinke.com

Marie Kane's poetry has been nominated three times for a Pushcart Prize and has appeared in many journals and anthologies. She is the 2006 Pennsylvania Bucks County Poet Laureate. Her chapbook, *Survivors in the Garden* (Big Table Publishing, 2012), mostly concerns life with multiple sclerosis. Her full-length collection, *Beauty, You Drive a Hard Bargain,* was released in 2017 by Kelsay Books. www.mariekanepoetry.com

198 / Schuylkill Valley Journal

Rob Kaniuk worked in the trades for the past 15 years. He started jotting notes and short poems at work and kept writing. After coming through a long and tumultuous history of drug use and poor decisions, he began to share what he'd been hiding for years.

Marilyn L. T. Klimcho is a poet and short story writer, with one nomination for a Pushcart Prize under her belt and a membership in Berks Bards, Inc. a grassroots poetry group centered in Reading, Pennsylvania where she lives with her husband, Patrick.

Judy Kronenfeld's fourth full-length collection of poetry, *Bird Flying through the Banquet*, was published by FutureCycle Press in 2017. Her prior books include *Shimmer* (WordTech, 2012) and *Light Lowering in Diminished Sevenths*, 2nd edition (Antrim House, 2012).

Peter Kuklinski is a native of Roxborough-Manayunk and presently lives in Bala Cynwyd. Peter is the Vice President of MTL, a Pennsylvania manufacturer of high quality woven furnishing textiles and is a past winner of the Santa Fe Writers Project and participant in the Summer Literary Seminar in St. Petersburg, Russia. His writings have appeared in *Modern Magazine* and the *Cosmopolitan Review*.

Richard Luftig is a former professor of educational psychology and special education at Miami University in Ohio now residing in California. He is a recipient of the Cincinnati Post-Corbett Foundation Award for Literature. His poems have appeared in numerous literary journals in the United States and internationally in Canada, Australia, Europe, and Asia. Two of his poems recently appeared in the anthology *Ten Years of Dos Madres Press*.

Joyce Meyers' books include *The Way Back* (Kelsay Books, 2017*)*, and two chapbooks, *Shapes of Love* (Finishing Line Press, 2010) and *Wild Mushrooms* (Plan B Press, 2007). Her work appears in *Atlanta Review*, *The Comstock Review*, *Iodine Poetry Journal*, and *Slant*. In 2014 she won the *Atlanta Review* International Poetry Competition and was nominated for a Pushcart Prize.

Diana Loercher Pazicky taught English and American literature as an Assistant Professor for twelve years at Temple University. Since her recent retirement, she has devoted her efforts to writing poetry and plays.

She is the author of *Cultural Orphans in America,* a social and political study of orphan imagery in early American literature.

Joseph Rathgeber is an author, poet, high school English teacher, and adjunct professor from New Jersey. His story collection is *The Abridged Autobiography of Yousef R. and Other Stories* (ELJ Publications, 2014). His work of hybrid poetry is *MJ* (Another New Calligraphy, 2015). He is a five-time Pushcart Prize nominee, recipient of a 2014 New Jersey State Council on the Arts Fellowship (Poetry), and a 2016 National Endowment for the Arts Creative Writing Fellowship (Prose).

Tree Riesener is the author of *Sleepers Awake,* a collection of fiction, winner of the Eludia Award (Sowilo Press), *The Hubble Cantos* (Aldrich Press), and *EK* (Cervena Barva Press). *Angel Fever,* a chapbook, will be published by Ravenna Press as part of their Triple series. *Quodlibet* will be published in 2018 by Diaphanous Press. Three previous chapbooks are *Liminalog, Angel Poison* and *Inscapes.* Her website is www.treeriesener. com. She is on Twitter and Facebook and loves to hear from readers.

Jacob Riyeff lives in Milwaukee with his wife and three children. His translation of *The Old English Rule of St. Benedict* (Cistercian Pub) will appear later this year, and his translation of Swami Abhishiktananda's collected poems will appear next year (Resource Pub).

This year, **Daniel Simpson** and his wife, Ona Gritz, collaborated on two books. Finishing Line Press published *Border Songs: A Conversation in Poems* this September. In January, Diode Editions will release *More Challenges for the Delusional: Peter Murphy's Prompts and the Writing They Inspired,* which Dan and Ona co-edited. Daniel Simpson's collection of poems, *School for the Blind,* was published in 2014 by Poets Wear Prada. His work has appeared in *Prairie Schooner, The Cortland Review, Beauty Is A Verb: The New Poetry of Disability, The New York Times,* and elsewhere. The recipient of a Fellowship in Literature from the Pennsylvania Council on the Arts, he served, along with Ona Gritz, as Poetry Editor for *Referential Magazine,* an online literary journal, from 2013 to 2016. His blog, *Inside the Invisible,* can be found at www.insidetheinvisible. wordpress.com.

Valentina Sinkevich, a Russian émigré poet, is a survivor of the forced labor camps set up by Germany during World War II. Her work has appeared in many Russian and American journals. She is the author of seven books of poetry and three books of memoirs. For thirty years she was the editor and publisher of the Russian poetry journal, *Vstrechi (Encounters)*. She was a long-time friend of the famous Russian poet, Yevgeny Yevtushenko. After Yevtushenko's death, Valentina's essay went "viral" in Russia.

Melody Smith lives in Ithaca, New York. She enjoys writing, supporting local musicians, and hiking. Currently, she is attending The College at Brockport, majoring in English. This is her first publication.

Robert Zaller is Distinguished University Professor of History Emeritus at Drexel University. His most recent books are *Robinson Jeffers and the American Sublime* and *Speaking to Power: Poems*.

Schuylkill Valley Journal
—Submission Guidelines—

The *Schuylkill Valley Journal* is published as both a print and online journal. The SVJ Print is released twice a year, in spring and fall. The SVJ Online (svjlit.com) is published on a more frequent basis. The SVJ publishes short stories, flash fiction, interviews, photography, citscapes, critical essays and features on art and sculpture (especially Philadelphia sculpture). The SVJ also publishes poetry; however, all poetry will first appear in the Print SVJ.

All submissions should be sent though the online website query.svj@gmail.com. We prefer previously unpublished work though published work is acceptable (indicate where previously published). Simultaneous submissions are OK (please notify us if your work is published elsewhere). All submissions will be considered for both our print and online journals. Our aim in reviewing material that is first considered for the SVJ Online (material other than poetry and longer short stores) is to inform writers of the status of their inquiry within two weeks.

Submissions should be sent in .doc or .rtf file format only in Times New Roman, 12 point font, and single-spaced and should include title, author name, bio and complete text, including any notes regarding previous publication. In the subject line all submissions should state the submission type (e.g., short story, flash fiction, poetry) and include the writer's full name, *and* contact information. Any file not meeting these specifications may not be read. Manuscripts will not be returned. All submissions except poetry should include a word count.

Poetry: Send 3-5 poems. Submit poetry to PoetrySVJ@gmail.com in the body of an email. The poetry co-editors are Bernadette McBride and Bill Wunder. If for some reason you are unable to submit via email, poetry can also be submitted via the SVJ website (svjlit.com).

Short Stories and Flash Fiction: 1-2 stories (if more than 3,000 words please only submit one). Flash fiction (preferably 500-1,000 words); short stories no more than 6,000 words. Submissions will be considered for both the online and print journal, with the exception of short stories greater than 2,000 words (Print SVJ only). We like fiction that tells a story or illuminates a character. We look for original use of language, fresh voices and diversity. We also seek writers who have insights into the mysteries of everyday life, relationships and the world around us. Stories can pose questions and answer them or not; however, they must be well-crafted. Stories can be sent through the online website at query.svj@gmail.com or can be sent via snail mail. The preferred method is via snail mail. Stories sent by snail mail should be typed, double-spaced, one side only with name, address, word count and bio on first page. Send to:

> Fran Metzman
> Fiction Editor, Schuylkill Valley Journal
> 1900 JFK Blvd, /2012
> Philadelphia, PA 19103

Essays and Interviews: 5,000 words max. (preferably under 2,000 words for the SVJ Online) on topics of literary or artistic interest, personal reflections, interviews, etc.). Submissions should incude the word count and bio on first page. Inquiry to email address (macpoet1@aol.com) is always advisable. Queries should include a concept/abstract of the proposed article, approximately a paragraph. All submissions will be sent through query.svj@gmail.com. All articles and non-fiction pieces will be assigned by editor.

—Copyright—

—Payment—

For contributors to the SVJ Print, payment is one copy of the journal in which your work appears. Additional copies are $10 each. All rights revert to authors upon publication. The cost of the Schuylkill Valley Journal is $10 an issue and $13 if sent via mail. For other information about the journal, contact Peter Krok, the publisher and Editor-in-Chief of the SVJ, and Humanities Director of the Manayunk-Roxborough Art Center (MRAC), at macpoet1@aol.com or by phone at 215-482-3363 (MRAC) or 610-609-1490 (cell).

—Subscription Form—
Schuylkill Valley Journal

Name: _____

Street Address:_____

City, State, Zip Code: _____

Phone: _____

Subscriptions: ( ) One Year $23*   ( ) Two Years $45*
                  (includes postage)   (includes postage)

For an issue that contains my work:
( ) Send my payment copies with my subscription copy.
( ) Send my payment copies and transfer my subscription to
     the next issue.

Contributions
     ( ) $10   ( ) $25   ( ) $50   ( ) $100   ( ) Other

Please make checks payable to
Peter Krok – Schuylkill Valley Journal
and mail to:
Peter Krok, 240 Golf Hills Road, Havertown, PA 19083

*For subscriptions that do not require postage, a one year subscription is $20 and a two year subscription is $40.

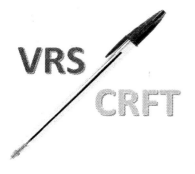